AIR CAMPAIGN

Normandy 1944

The 'Transportation Plan' to cut D-Day communications

JULIAN HALE | ILLUSTRATED BY GRAHAM TURNER

OSPREY PUBLISHING
Bloomsbury Publishing Plc
Kemp House, Chawley Park, Cumnor Hill, Oxford OX2 9PH, UK
Bloomsbury Publishing Ireland Limited,
29 Earlsfort Terrace, Dublin 2, D02 AY28, Ireland
1385 Broadway, 5th Floor, New York, NY 10018, USA
E-mail: info@ospreypublishing.com
www.ospreypublishing.com

OSPREY is a trademark of Osprey Publishing Ltd

First published in Great Britain in 2025

© Osprey Publishing Ltd, 2025

All rights reserved. No part of this publication may be: i) reproduced or transmitted in any form, electronic or mechanical, including photocopying, recording or by means of any information storage or retrieval system without prior permission in writing from the publishers; or ii) used or reproduced in any way for the training, development or operation of artificial intelligence (AI) technologies, including generative AI technologies. The rights holders expressly reserve this publication from the text and data mining exception as per Article 4(3) of the Digital Single Market Directive (EU) 2019/790.

A catalogue record for this book is available from the British Library.

ISBN: PB 9781472865809; eBook 9781472865830;
ePDF 9781472865816; XML 9781472865823

25 26 27 28 29 10 9 8 7 6 5 4 3 2 1

Maps by www.bounford.com
Diagrams by Adam Tooby
3D BEVs by Paul Kime
Index by Fionbar Lyons
Typeset by PDQ Digital Media Solutions, Bungay, UK
Printed by Repro India Ltd.

Title page: see p.15.

Osprey Publishing supports the Woodland Trust, the UK's leading woodland conservation charity.

To find out more about our authors and books visit www.ospreypublishing.com. Here you will find extracts, author interviews, details of forthcoming events and the option to sign up for our newsletter.

For product safety related questions contact productsafety@bloomsbury.com

Author's acknowledgements:
Thanks are due to the National Archives and the University of East Anglia Archives and Special Collections, Andrew Dennis, RAF Museum Library and Archive and Stuart Hadaway and Lee Barton of the RAF Air Historical Branch. The French Railways Society, Christian Wolmar and Ian Thirsk all helped freely with research. Dr Emma Riley and others were kind enough to comment on various parts of the manuscript. I am grateful to Osprey's Tom Milner for his help and patience during this book's preparation.

AIR CAMPAIGN

CONTENTS

INTRODUCTION	4
CHRONOLOGY	6
ATTACKER'S CAPABILITIES	10
DEFENDER'S CAPABILITIES	21
CAMPAIGN OBJECTIVES	31
THE CAMPAIGN	49
AFTERMATH AND ANALYSIS	88
FURTHER READING	93
INDEX	95

INTRODUCTION

The history of all coalitions is a tale of the reciprocal complaints of allies.

Winston Churchill, *Marlborough: His Life and Times*

Railways are the arteries of modern armies. Vitality decreases when they are blocked, and terminates when they are permanently severed.

Charles à Court Repington, *Imperial Strategy*

Stalin inscrutable, Roosevelt patrician, Churchill reduced: the 'Big Three' meet at Tehran, December 1943. The promise to Stalin of an invasion in Spring, 1944 put enormous pressure on the Western Allies, none more than those formulating a pre-invasion plan for the air forces. (Pictures From History/UIG/Getty Images)

On 9 April 1944, it seemed that the inhabitants of Lille had much to look forward to. Although the city in north-east France had been under German occupation for almost four years, the possibility of liberation looked ever more likely. Furthermore, despite Lille's importance as a major coal and railway centre, it had thus far not suffered any Allied bombing raids.

As the daylight faded, the overcast which had shrouded much of northern France dispersed, leaving Lille bathed in the light of a three-quarter moon. The townspeople were unaware that at midnight, 130 miles to the south, RAF heavy bombers had begun a devastating attack on the major Villeneuve St Georges marshalling yard on the outskirts of Paris. Nor did they know that the pathfinder Mosquitoes, which had opened the attack, were now heading towards their own city. At around 40 minutes past midnight, the first Target Indicator bombs burst in a spectacular display over the Déliverance rail yard, located in the western Lille suburb of Lomme.

Over the next 30 minutes, 227 Halifaxes and Lancasters dropped over 1,050 tons of bombs. About 50 bombs fell in the goods yard itself, where they cut all the through-lines, destroyed an estimated 2,124 goods wagons and blew up an ammunition train. The after-mission report noted, in passing, that some industrial premises adjacent to the yard, engaged in textile manufacture, were destroyed.

In truth, much of the bombing had spread beyond the yard itself and fallen among suburban housing. Around 5,000 homes were destroyed or damaged and 456 French men, women and children killed. War had come to the people of Lille that night, in its most brutal and terrifying form. It would do so again and again, to scores of towns across northern France and Belgium, before liberation finally came.

Ten months earlier, on 10 June 1943, the Pointblank directive was issued to the British and American strategic bomber forces, directing them to engage in 'the progressive destruction and dislocation of the German military, industrial and economic system, and the undermining of the morale of the German people to a point where their capacity for armed resistance is fatally weakened'. The directive added, 'whenever Allied Armies re-enter the Continent, you will afford all possible support in the manner most effective.' Few, be they British, American or German, doubted a cross-Channel invasion would almost certainly come in the spring of 1944. However, if the Third Reich's industrial base or the morale of its population could be 'fatally weakened' by bombing alone, then so much the better. When the 'Big Three' – Franklin Roosevelt, Winston Churchill and Josef Stalin – met at Tehran in late November 1943, the chief result was a definite date for *Overlord*: the re-entry to Europe in May 1944. From this point on, the countdown began and the date for the invasion promised to Stalin by the two Western leaders was to draw ever nearer.

A night photograph of Lille-Déliverance taken on 10–11 April by a Lancaster of No. 61 Squadron. Although the photograph hints at the confusing picture such raids offered, it can be seen that the bombing is scattering over the suburbs of Lomme and Le Marais. (Crown Copyright, MoD)

An outward appearance of Anglo–American unanimity served to mask some serious cracks. The planning and conduct of the pre-*Overlord* air campaign inherited tensions which ran across national, strategic, service and even personal boundaries. The story would involve a large cast of senior politicians, ambitious airmen and egocentric intelligence experts, scientists and economists, some of whom proved willing to engage in exhausting and vituperative debates over a range of issues. Who should command the tactical air forces? Should the strategic air forces even participate in *Overlord* operations and, if so, for how long? If the heavy bombers were to be used, who would control them, and with what degree of authority? Would the bombing cause too many French casualties – and what constituted 'too many'? Finally, was the plan eventually adopted even the right one – or should an alternative be sought?

The concept eventually adopted, the Transportation Plan, proposed a concerted offensive against the railway facilities of northern France and Belgium by the Allied air forces. As the campaign progressed, it was subjected to a series of changes, which almost certainly reduced its overall effectiveness. Moreover, the overlapping tension between the continuing Pointblank directive and *Overlord* was never fully resolved. Eventually, another campaign, an American-led proposal to cripple the German petrol, oil and lubrication industry, began in May 1944 as the Transportation Plan was reaching its height.

Many air campaigns have been mired in strategic and moral controversy, both at the time and in subsequent years. The Transportation Plan is no exception. Although some of those involved left their own memoirs, the polarisation produced by the campaign from its inception means they are inevitably compromised by their writers' own partisanship. Few historians have since tackled the subject in its entirety. The campaign therefore exists in a sort of forlorn historiographical wilderness, overshadowed by the Combined Bomber Offensive on one side and the liberation of Europe on the other. It is to be hoped that this book will go some way to changing that view.

CHRONOLOGY

1938
1 January The French railway companies are nationalized to form the *Société nationale des chemins de fer français* (SNCF).

1940
The French and Belgian railways become subject to German control. Over the next four years, large quantities of locomotives, stock and other supplies are requisitioned by Germany.

1942
While an advisor to Combined Operations, Solly Zuckerman draws up the air bombardment plan for Operation *Blazing*, a proposal for an unrealised commando raid on Alderney in the Channel Islands.

1943
15 March–11 May 1944 Operation *Strangle* targets a range of railway facilities and bridges in Italy. The bombing continues into late June in support of Operation *Diadem*, the fourth battle of Monte Cassino.

10 June The Pointblank directive is issued, outlining the priorities for the Combined Bomber Offensive. The primary objectives are the 'destruction and dislocation of the German military, industrial and economic system', with the Luftwaffe as the priority for the US Eighth Air Force.

11 June Operation *Corkscrew*, a ten-day air bombardment of Pantelleria between Sicily and Tunisia, based on planning by Zuckerman and others, results in the island's surrender.

June–July Zuckerman proposes attacking the 'nodal points' of the Sicilian railway system during the invasion of the island (Operation *Husky*).

16 November The directive assigning Leigh-Mallory the command of the Allied Expeditionary Air Force (AEAF) is issued. The last paragraph stated, 'Directives as to the control of the strategic air forces will follow at a later date. In the meantime … you should, during the preparatory period, exercise operational control of the air forces under your command in such a manner as to lend maximum support to the Strategic Air Force offensive.' Discussions begin over control of the strategic air forces for *Overlord*.

28 November–1 December The Tehran Conference. Churchill and Roosevelt state that Operation *Overlord* will be launched in May 1944, a date subsequently changed to June 1944. Pointblank's objectives have yet to be fulfilled.

December Eisenhower is chosen by Roosevelt as the Supreme Allied Commander. He is adamant that he must be given control of all the air forces, including Bomber Command and the US strategic air forces.

The first Operation *Crossbow* attacks on V-1 flying bomb sites begin. These continue through the spring of 1944.

Air Chief Marshal Sir Arthur Tedder and Solly Zuckerman return to Britain from the Mediterranean theatre. Tedder is appointed Deputy to the Supreme Commander.

28 December Zuckerman's report on the bombing of six Italian rail centres is produced and forms the basis for the Transportation Plan of 1944.

30 December The Allied Joint Planning Staff produce 'Study No. 6: The Delay of Enemy Reserves during the Initial Stages of Neptune' (*Neptune* being the naval component of *Overlord*).

1944
13 January Air Chief Marshal Sir Arthur Harris writes that although *Overlord* 'must be regarded as an inescapable commitment', Bomber Command was incapable of mounting operations in direct support of the invasion.

22 January The Transportation Plan is discussed at the sixth meeting of the AEAF Bombing Committee. Zuckerman's concept calls for the contribution of the heavy bomber fleets of both Britain and the United States. Despite some reservations, the general mood of the meeting is that the plan, in principle, is satisfactory. Both Tedder and Leigh-Mallory are supporters of Zuckerman's plan.

1 February The process of merging the Transportation Plan with the Initial Joint Plan (the overall plan for *Overlord*) begins.

12 February The third draft of the Transportation Plan is produced.

13 February A new directive renews the priority of Pointblank.

17 February The American Enemy Objectives Unit (EOU) produces a paper suggesting that an 'interdiction' campaign, targeting bridges and German supply depots, would produce a greater effect with smaller effort and fewer civilian casualties than Zuckerman's Transportation Plan.

20–25 February Operation *Argument*. The US strategic air forces and their escorting fighters engage the Luftwaffe in a series of missions targeting the German aircraft industry. Nearly 100 Luftwaffe pilots are killed. The American air forces begin to win the battle for air superiority over Germany.

25 February A meeting of the key players is held, in order that Tedder might gain the support of Harris and Spaatz. Both make clear their opposition to any deviation from the Combined Bomber Offensive.

'PANTELLERIA FALLS: CAPITULATION FOLLOWS 1,000 PLANE ONSLAUGHT.' The capture of the tiny island of Pantelleria in 1943 came after an air plan devised by Solly Zuckerman and his staff. Zuckerman's star was now in the ascendant. (John Frost Newspapers/Alamy Stock Photo)

29 February A meeting attended by Winston Churchill, Portal and Eisenhower clarifies the issue of command of the strategic air forces in the run-up to *Overlord*. Eisenhower would be given control over the bomber forces, via Tedder, in the 'tactical phase' before the assault. All agree that the objective of gaining air superiority over the Luftwaffe should be pursued concurrently with the Transportation Plan.

5 March In the aftermath of Operation *Argument*, the EOU produces a report which rejects the Transportation Plan, instead suggesting a concerted campaign against German synthetic oil production. Spaatz is soon convinced and prepares to suggest the Oil Plan as an alternative to the Transportation Plan.

6–7 March Bomber Command begins the campaign when it makes an experimental raid on the French railway centre at Trappes. Further attacks are made during the following week on the rail centres at Le Mans and Amiens.

25 March At a meeting to decide on the campaign before *Overlord*, Eisenhower adjudicates between Tedder's proposal for the Transportation Plan and Spaatz's advocacy of the Oil Plan. Spaatz does not mention the proposal for the interdiction campaign to be undertaken alongside the oil campaign. Eisenhower sides with Tedder. Portal concedes that oil attacks would be worth attempting when the first crisis of *Overlord* has passed.

27 March The directive giving Eisenhower direction of the Allied strategic air forces is issued.

5 April A War Cabinet Defence Committee meeting discusses the Transportation Plan. Although neither Churchill nor many in the Cabinet support the plan, they agree that it should go ahead for the time being.

10–11 April Bomber Command attacks Tours, Tergnier, Laon, Aulnoye and Ghent with 789 bombers, 19 of which are lost.

12 April Under pressure from Churchill, a revised list of rail targets is issued by the AEAF, excluding two Parisian rail centres, the bombing of which would produce heavy civilian casualties.

The major *Region Nord* railway centre at Aulnoye, north-eastern France, before the attack on 10–11 April 1944. The complex of servicing and maintenance facilities are at the top of the image, then the receiving tracks. The large and apparently busy classification yard is below, in the centre of the photograph. The through-lines are visible at the bottom. (Crown Copyright, MoD)

15 April Eisenhower as Supreme Commander and Tedder as his Deputy assume control over the strategic air forces.

17 April The first directive is issued by Eisenhower for the Transportation Plan. It restates the priority of targeting the German aircraft industry and the gaining of air superiority, offering Spaatz considerable leeway in target selection.

20–21 April La Chapelle in Paris is attacked in the first major test over a railway centre of the No. 5 Group marking method. The attack is accurate and well-concentrated. La Chapelle is so badly damaged it is not attacked again.

25 April Hawker Typhoons of the RAF's Second Tactical Air Force attack and damage a viaduct in the Cherbourg area, proving that it is possible for fighter-bombers to destroy or heavily damage bridges.

26 April Another meeting of the War Cabinet Defence Committee. Churchill resolves to refer the Transportation Plan to the whole War Cabinet on 27 April. If the War Cabinet expresses its opposition to the campaign's continuation, Churchill will telegram President Roosevelt for his views.

29 April Churchill urges Eisenhower to abandon the campaign and refers to a plan by the Directorate of Bomber Operations to attack bridges and supply depots. Eisenhower refuses to abandon the campaign but does agree to suspend attacks against twenty-seven of the rail centres in heavily populated areas.

1 May The US Eighth Air Force begins its campaign with attacks on railway centres in eastern France and western Germany.

5 May Eisenhower lifts the targets suspension imposed on 29 April.

6 May Leigh-Mallory sanctions interdiction attacks on bridges by fighters and medium bombers.

7 May US Ninth Air Force P-47 Thunderbolt fighter-bombers successfully attack the bridge at Vernon, on the River Seine. On the same day, Churchill telegrams Roosevelt, as per his announcement on 26 April.

10 May Leigh-Mallory orders more bridge-cutting attacks to be made by fighters and medium bombers of the Ninth Air Force. A few days later, attacks on the Seine bridges cease in order to avoid compromising security for D-Day. Attacks begin against bridges to the east.

11 May Roosevelt replies to Churchill's telegram, writing that he was 'not prepared to impose from this distance any restriction on military action'.

20 May Confident that most French and Belgian rail traffic was now devoted to German military needs, Leigh-Mallory sanctions fighter-bomber sweeps against trains on open lines.

21 May Large numbers of Allied fighters fan out across France and Belgium, damaging over 100 railway locomotives. The operation becomes known as 'Chattanooga Choo Choo Day'. Before D-Day, five more Chattanooga Days are flown across France, Germany and even Poland.

24 May Attacks recommence on the Seine bridges.

26 May The German transport authority orders a reduction in rail journeys by day. German locomotive crews substitute for French crews on the more hazardous routes.

5 June The seven Seine bridges selected for attack are cut on the eve of D-Day.

6 June Attacks begin on the eight bridges across the Loire. The establishment of two lines of interdiction.

7–8 June Bomber Command loses 28 from 337 aircraft in attacks on rail centres around Paris.

23 and 28 June Two important supply routes are reopened into Normandy by the Germans.

June–July The Seine and Loire bridges selected for attack are alternately cut, repaired and re-cut.

Late July Operation *Cobra*, the US breakout from the Normandy bridgehead, is materially assisted by the collapse of the German logistical network on the Loire.

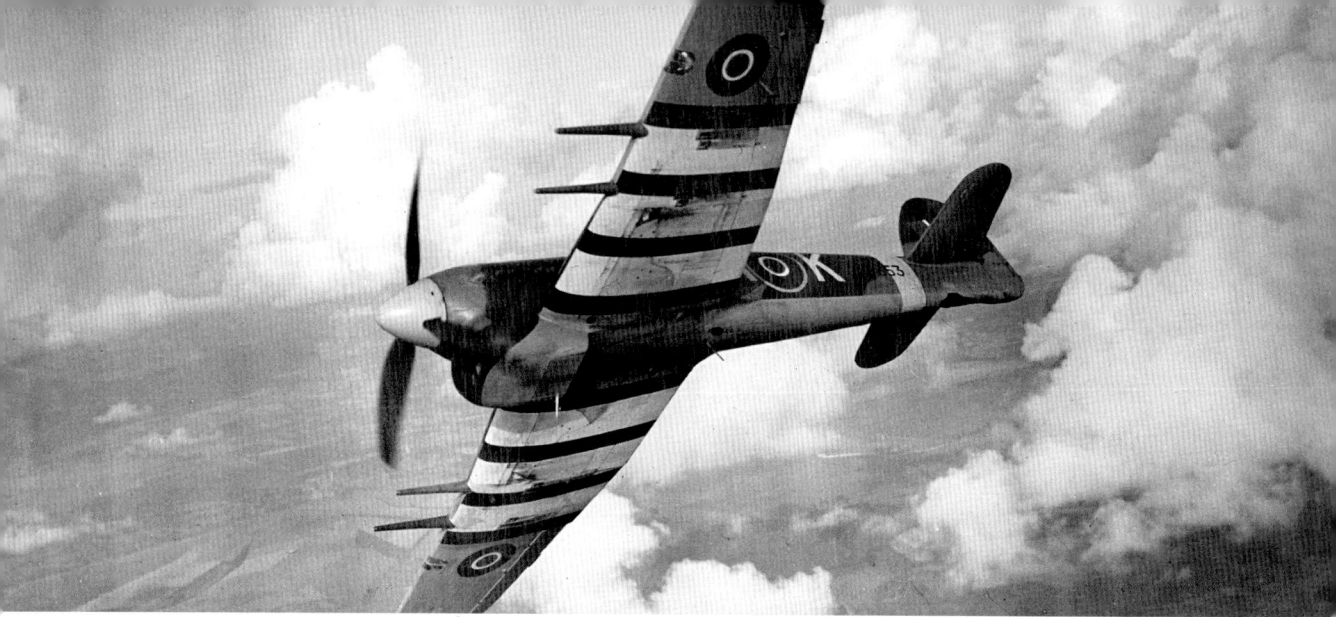

ATTACKER'S CAPABILITIES

The Hawker Typhoon, famous in the ground-attack role, proved the feasibility of bridge attacks by fighter-bombers. Although attacks on German transport and armour certainly exerted some influence later in the campaign, more recent research has downplayed previous conclusions concerning their effectiveness. (Crown Copyright, MoD)

The process of uniting the Anglo-American war effort was a long and complex one, criss-crossed by a complex pattern of political, professional and personal differences. By 1944, most – if not all – of these differences between the British and American air forces had been settled in the Mediterranean. An incident which illustrates this occurred in North Africa in the summer of 1943 and was later recounted by Solly Zuckerman. During a meeting at General Carl Spaatz's USAAF headquarters, Air Chief Marshal Arthur Coningham (commanding the RAF's Desert Air Force) suddenly left the room and went into the garden. 'We could see him picking blossoms from a hibiscus bush,' Zuckerman wrote. 'He then returned and bent down on one knee in front of Tooey [Spaatz's nickname] saying, as he proffered the flowers, "Master, I bring you these." Tooey was not amused.'

Organization

The organization charged with executing *Overlord*, Supreme Headquarters Allied Expeditionary Force (SHAEF), was the child of two parents. Allied Forces Headquarters had been the joint command post in the Mediterranean theatre, while in the UK, Headquarters, Chief of Staff to the Supreme Allied Commander (COSSAC) had been charged with planning *Overlord* since spring 1943. The marriage of these two organizations inevitably produced tensions. Given this, it was indeed fortunate that President Roosevelt chose General Dwight D. Eisenhower as the AEF's Supreme Commander. Montgomery's typically crisp dismissal of Eisenhower ('nice chap, no soldier') unwittingly reveals Eisenhower's greatest attribute: his genius for team management. In February 1944, the Luftwaffe's historical branch acutely observed:

> He leaves the initiative to his subordinates whom he manages to inspire to supreme efforts through kind understanding and easy discipline. His strongest point is said to be an ability for adjusting personalities to one another and smoothing over opposite viewpoints. Eisenhower enjoys the greatest popularity with Roosevelt and Churchill.

In his previous role as Supreme Commander in the Mediterranean, Eisenhower had formed close links with his senior air commanders, Air Chief Marshal Sir Arthur Tedder and Spaatz. Tedder first made his name in 1941–42, heading RAF Middle East Command, where he was instrumental in moulding the forces under his command into a cohesive whole. Tedder and Arthur Coningham devoted much effort to improving air support for the armies in North Africa. From 1943, the development of a unified air force attuned to the needs of the ground forces, and the need for close Anglo-American relations, remained at the heart of Tedder's approach. The Luftwaffe historical branch noted:

> Tedder is on good terms with Eisenhower, to whom he is superior in both intelligence and energy… He is very popular with the troops on account of his consideration and unassuming appearance. Obviously, we are dealing here with one of the most eminent personalities amongst the invasion leaders.

The Chief of the Air Staff, Sir Charles Portal, carried a great deal of authority as the professional head of the RAF. Portal instructed Harris to experiment with the attacks of early March 1944 and argued in favour of the Transportation Plan at the end of the same month. (Crown Copyright, MoD)

Tedder was no stranger to personal tragedy. His wife died in an air crash near Cairo in 1943 and their eldest son had been killed over France in August 1940.

Tedder owed a debt to Air Chief Marshal Sir Charles Portal, Chief of the Air Staff since late 1940. A key moment had come in late 1941 when Churchill, dismayed by the failure to gain a decisive victory in North Africa, sought to dismiss Tedder as C-in-C RAF Middle East. Portal, confident in Tedder's abilities, was instrumental in securing the latter's position. As Chief of the Air Staff, Portal was the agent of the Combined Chiefs of Staff for the control of the Combined Bomber Offensive. Portal recognised that Pointblank was the preparation for an invasion and not, as some believed, an alternative. As such, he would wield a great deal of influence in the forthcoming discussions concerning *Overlord*.

The Chief of Staff of the USAAF was General Henry 'Hap' Arnold, whose position was roughly analogous to that of Portal. As a member of both the US Joint Chiefs of Staff and the Allied Combined Chiefs of Staff, Arnold provided strategic direction to the USAAF in Britain and support and advice to their commander, General Carl Spaatz.

Carl 'Tooey' Spaatz (the nickname derived from his resemblance to a schoolmate, Francis J. Toohey) qualified as a pilot in 1916. In 1929, he had been part of the crew (which included Ira Eaker, who went on to command the US Eighth Air Force, and Elwood Quesada, who later led XIX Fighter Command) of the *Question Mark*, an aircraft which used air-to-air refuelling to establish a record of 150 hours in the air. Following a brief period as commander of the Eighth Air Force, Spaatz led US air forces in the Mediterranean. In January 1944, Spaatz returned to the UK when he was given control of the US Strategic Air Forces (USSTAF) in Europe. This umbrella command exerted operational control of the Eighth Air Force and administrative control of the Ninth Air Force in the UK, and the Twelfth and Fifteenth Air Forces in the Mediterranean. This made Spaatz a formidably powerful player, who could also count on the support of 'Hap' Arnold, particularly in his forthcoming struggle to maintain the political and operational independence of the USSTAF.

Intelligence

The planning for the coming campaign would be subjected to scrutiny and advice from a complex bureaucracy of several British (and one American) intelligence agencies which had variously participated in the collection, interpretation and dissemination of intelligence during the previous three-and-a-half years of the air war against Germany. Those who interpreted the mass of intelligence which flowed into Britain were considered experts in their respective fields, and their opinions carried a good deal of weight.

The Ministry of Economic Warfare's (MEW) Economic Objectives Department, headed by Oliver Lawrence, advised and assessed Bomber Command's offensive in terms of its

General Henry 'Hap' Arnold, the US Army Air Forces Chief of Staff, based in Washington, was a strong ally for Spaatz in the UK. Both men foresaw that a decisive contribution by the air force in 1944 would ease the path to independence in the post-war years. (Photo12/UIG/Getty Images)

An anatomist by profession, Solly Zuckerman led studies of bomb damage during the Blitz and in 1944, became the principal architect of the Transportation Plan. A highly intelligent man of forthright views, Zuckerman was responsible for the conclusions of the post-war British Bombing Survey Report, which defended the plan he had designed. (Fox Photos/Hulton Archive/Getty Images)

economic effect on the German war effort. The MEW had close links to the American Enemy Objectives Unit. Lt Col Richard D'Oyly Hughes, the head of the EOU, wrote, 'This vast British agency was busily engaged in producing voluminous studies covering every conceivable facet of the economies and industries of the Axis countries. What seemed like a truck load of paper emerged from their offices every day.'

American intelligence relied on the already-established British agencies throughout the war. Anglo-American co-operation worked well at this level and during 1942 and 1943, USAAF officers filled numerous positions within the British agencies. The EOU, staffed by a very small team of economists, nominally came under the American Embassy in London. It was in fact an arm of the OSS (the Office of Strategic Services – the forerunner of the CIA) and was the de facto intelligence service for the USSTAF. The unit searched for target systems which were vital to the German war economy but simultaneously vulnerable to air attack. Some of the leading lights in the EOU were Charles Kindleberger, Carl Kaysen and Walt Rostow, all of whom would go on to hold high-level positions in Washington.

Other important players were the RAF's own service, Air Intelligence (AI), which among other duties, controlled the Photographic Reconnaissance Unit (PRU) and the associated Central Interpretation Unit (CIU) at RAF Medmenham in Buckinghamshire, which collected and evaluated all imagery taken over Occupied Europe.

The Railway Research Service (RRS), under the Ministry of Home Security, was headed by E. D. Brant and C. E. R. Sherrington. These experts had evaluated German attacks on Britain's railway system during the Blitz; Zuckerman would lean on their knowledge in preparing his plan in 1944. Mention should also be made of Lord Cherwell (Professor Frederick Lindemann). 'The Prof' enjoyed a wide remit as Churchill's personal scientific advisor, and although not a member of the War Cabinet, he usually attended its meetings.

Solly Zuckerman, a respected anatomist, had been employed to research the effects of bombing during the Luftwaffe's Blitz on Britain. Zuckerman locked horns with Professor Lindemann in 1942, when he expressed scepticism over the value of area bombing. Zuckerman was later added as a scientific advisor to Tedder's staff in the Mediterranean. In this role, he drew up the plan for the bombing of Pantelleria – a small island deemed by defenders and attackers alike to be impregnable. The lengthy series of air attacks forced the garrison's surrender, putting Zuckerman's star firmly in the ascendant. In late 1943, Zuckerman compiled a study of the air campaign against the Sicilian and southern Italian railway systems, before returning to the UK as scientific advisor to Tedder. Zuckerman's cleverness (and intellectual vanity) could be infuriating, especially to senior airmen with their own entrenched ideas. Yet Zuckerman, Tedder and Spaatz were friends, and remained so, despite the storms of the pre-*Overlord* controversies.

The Allied Expeditionary Air Force – a united air force?

The planning for *Overlord* was complicated by an assumption that the crucial battle for air superiority would be fought over the beachhead. Concurrent experience in the Mediterranean showed that fighter-bomber support both before and during a landing was essential. It was therefore decided that an Allied Expeditionary Air Force (AEAF) should be created to co-ordinate Anglo-American tactical operations, under an experienced fighter commander. The AEAF assumed control over two organizations: Fighter Command, renamed Air Defence of Great Britain, maintained responsibility for home defence, while the Second Tactical Air Force (2nd TAF) conducted cross-Channel operations. The 2nd TAF comprised the medium bombers of No. 2 Group Bomber Command, two fighter-bomber Groups (Nos 83 and 84) drawn from Fighter Command, plus other ancillary units. The US Ninth Air Force, under Brereton, would come under the AEAF umbrella in November 1943.

Some of the key figures gathered at Supreme Headquarters, Allied Expeditionary Force. Both Eisenhower and Tedder (front row) played a key role in maintaining Allied unanimity, Montgomery (right) and Leigh-Mallory (back row) less so – although the latter's subsequent reputation is not entirely deserved. (Bettmann/Getty Images)

The AEAF was to be commanded by Air Chief Marshal Sir Trafford Leigh-Mallory, a disputatious and unpopular figure who ultimately became marginalised among the Allied high command. Portal had sponsored Leigh-Mallory for the AEAF position because of his experience as the former C-in-C of RAF Fighter Command, as well as his knowledge of army co-operation. It is notable that while many airmen in the SHAEF hierarchy were veterans from the Mediterranean theatre, Leigh-Mallory was an exception.

Part of Leigh-Mallory's unpopularity within the RAF stemmed from his clashes with Air Vice Marshal Keith Park, commander of the RAF's No.11 Group, during the Battle of Britain. American colleagues thought Leigh-Mallory 'haughty' and 'naïve'. During a planning meeting held on 25 March 1944, Leigh-Mallory reputedly expressed a reluctance to go down to posterity as the man who killed thousands of Frenchmen, to which Air Chief Marshal Sir Arthur Harris is said to have retorted, 'What makes you think you're going to go down to posterity at all?'

Air Chief Marshal Sir Arthur Coningham, commanding the Second Tactical Air Force, was a friend and ally of Tedder from the North African campaign. Eisenhower thought highly of Coningham, describing him as 'impulsive, quick, earnest and sincere. He knows his job.'

Air Chief Marshal Sir Trafford Leigh-Mallory was given command of the Allied tactical air forces – but not the strategic bombers as he had originally hoped. Neither his personality nor his professional opinions endeared him to his British or American colleagues, and as *Overlord* approached, he cut an ever more isolated figure. (Imperial War Museums via Getty Images)

Aircraft

The 26 squadrons of Hawker Typhoons formed the backbone of the 2nd TAF. Although designed as an interceptor, the Typhoon's thick wing section limited maximum speed and the Napier Sabre engine did not offer competitive high-altitude performance. Instead, strong low-level performance, heavy armament and strong construction suited the 'Tiffy' to the ground-attack role. This was tempered by the liquid-cooled Sabre's vulnerability to ground fire, and the Typhoon squadrons suffering a heavy casualty rate to the end of the war. The newer Hawker Tempest resembled the Typhoon but in fact represented a major advance over its older stablemate. The Sabre-engined Tempest Mk V entered service with two squadrons in May 1944. Finally, the Supermarine Spitfire equipped almost as many squadrons in the 2nd TAF as the Typhoon, despite being ill-suited to the fighter-bomber role.

The US Ninth Air Force

The Ninth Air Force had its roots as the US Army Middle East Air Force; the Ninth supported the later stages of the North African campaign and the invasion of Sicily. In the reorganization of late 1943, the name was transferred to a nascent air force in the UK, using fighters and

Tactical air force commanders Air Marshal Sir Arthur Coningham (2nd TAF) and Lt General Brereton (Ninth Air Force) beam at the camera. Both had served together in the Mediterranean and were strong proponents of the value of tactical air operations. Neither was universally liked by their respective peers. (Imperial War Museums, CH 12783)

medium bombers passed down from the Eighth Air Force. Through much of early 1944, the Ninth remained short of equipment and many units found themselves operating from hastily completed airfields in the south of England. By D-Day, however, the Ninth had become a very powerful force indeed. It was created specifically to support *Overlord*, but was also expected to provide fighter support and diversionary raids for the Eighth Air Force's Pointblank missions.

The Ninth's commander, Lieutenant General Lewis Brereton, transferred from the Mediterranean theatre with the Ninth Air Force to prepare for *Overlord*. While the commander of the First US Army, General Omar Bradley, held Brereton in low regard both personally and professionally, Brereton found a kindred spirit in Coningham, his opposite number. Both men agreed on tactical issues, but unlike Coningham, Brereton enjoyed no aura stemming from past successes. Moreover, Brereton was regarded by some, including Spaatz, as something of a maverick, with ambitions for some sort of semi-independent role for the Ninth Air Force.

Lieutenant General Elwood 'Pete' Quesada had also served in North Africa, where he and Coningham had become firm allies. Quesada took command of the XIX Fighter Command element of the Ninth Air Force, and was to play an important role in promoting the later 'interdiction' campaign.

The Ninth Air Force's most numerous medium bomber, the Martin B-26 Marauder, had something of a chequered reputation, which stemmed from a relatively high wing loading and a consequent series of accidents among inexperienced crews in 1941. This earned the B-26 the 'Widow Maker' nickname, from which it never seemed to quite escape. While a host of changes on the production line were intended to improve the aircraft's safety, it was pilot training and experience which made the greatest difference. The eight B-26 Groups would go on to have the lowest attrition rate in the Ninth Air Force.

In late January 1944, after some wrangling between Brereton and Spaatz, it was decided that of the nine P-51 Mustang Groups scheduled for the ETO, the Eighth Air Force was to be awarded seven and the Ninth just two. Given the P-51's long-range, this decision made complete sense. In turn, the Ninth Air Force would operate 13 P-47 Thunderbolt Groups.

The Republic P-47 Thunderbolt evolved from a decision made in 1940 to create an interceptor with a heavy load of guns, ammunition, armour and fuel. Such a desire necessitated a large and powerful engine: the 2,000hp turbocharged Pratt & Whitney Double Wasp. Little consideration was given to weight-saving, and the result was a massive fighter of sturdy construction. The P-47B flew its first sorties with the Eighth Air Force in April 1943. The definitive P-47D began to join the Eighth and Ninth Air Forces from late 1943. Notably, the 'razorbacks' gradually began to be replaced by the bubble-canopied model in early 1944. Pilots learned to use the Thunderbolt's structural strength, steadiness as a gun platform and the heavy armament of bombs or rockets and eight .50cal machine guns to their advantage. It was these characteristics which gave the Thunderbolt its true vocation as a fighter-bomber.

By March 1944, the Mustang equipped three Eighth Air Force Fighter Groups and one Group of the Ninth Air Force. The Mustang's superb high-altitude performance and long range made it the obvious choice for the Eighth's penetrations into German territory. Despite the vulnerability of the liquid-cooled Merlin engine to ground fire, Mustangs were used extensively for strafing airfields, transport and other targets of opportunity.

The distinctive twin-engine Lockheed P-38 Lightning was originally intended as a long-range fighter. The aircraft performed best at high-altitude and was never as manoeuvrable as

This 365th Fighter Group Thunderbolt has belly-landed, possibly as a result of damage from ground-fire, sometime after D-Day. Despite their rugged build, the ground-attack P-47s of the Ninth Air Force suffered, like all fighter-bombers, at the hands of German light flak. (Imperial War Museums, FRE 6409)

its single-engined rivals. These problems notwithstanding, the aircraft was used with success in the ground-attack role. The Eighth Air Force deployed four Groups of P-38s and the Ninth Air Force three Groups from April 1944.

RAF Bomber Command

By early 1944, RAF Bomber Command had become almost unrecognisable from the feeble force which had begun operations against Germany in mid-1940. This was due in no small part to the efforts of its commander, Air Chief Marshal Sir Arthur Harris. Known as 'Bert' to his peers, 'Butch' to his crews and 'Bomber' by the British public, Harris was – and remains – a polarising figure. Like many senior British commanders, Harris's strategic outlook was coloured by the experience of World War I. In addition, 'under Churchill's protection', Zuckerman wrote, 'Harris had become almost a law unto himself'. Tedder voiced a similar opinion: 'Harris was by way of being something of a dictator who had very much the reputation of not taking too kindly to directions from outside his own command.'

The Pointblank directive gave the Allied strategic air forces the opportunity, at least theoretically, to obviate the need for an invasion of Europe. The directive also granted a great deal of flexibility in terms of target selection, which for Bomber Command often meant bombing German city centres. The prize remained Berlin, the destruction of which could, Harris claimed, prompt a German surrender. Whether Harris actually believed his own statement is another question. Nevertheless, between November 1943 and January 1944, Bomber Command made 14 attacks on Berlin, before turning to other major German cities in February and March. During this entire period, 1,117 bombers were lost, an average loss rate of 3.8 per cent.

Lockheed P-38J Lightnings of the 364th Fighter Group, Eighth Air Force, summer 1944. The Lightning was endowed with good range and, if damaged, could fly on one engine. The P-38 Groups of both Eighth and Ninth Air Forces participated in the Chattanooga operations in May and early June 1944. (Imperial War Museums, FRE 10101)

Aircraft

Bomber Command was divided into six main Groups ranged along the East Coast of England from Yorkshire to Suffolk: Nos 1, 3, 4, 5 and 6 (Canadian) Main Force Groups and 8 (Pathfinder) Group.

ATTACKER'S CAPABILITIES

A Hawker Tempest Mk V of 486 Squadron, April 1944. The earliest Tempests were distinguishable by their protruding 20mm cannon barrels. Like the Typhoon, the black and white stripes applied to the underside were to distinguish the Tempest from the Fw 190. The first Tempests began fighter sweeps and ground-attack missions shortly before D-Day. (Crown Copyright, MoD)

The Avro Lancaster remains the best known of Bomber Command's wartime aircraft. The Lancaster's qualities are well known and its modern reputation certainly overshadows its contemporaries. Nevertheless, the Lancaster could carry a heavier bombload higher, further and faster than either the Halifax or the Stirling – although the Halifax B.III was almost comparable in performance. The Lancaster fully equipped Nos 1 and 5 Groups. These had accordingly borne the brunt of the Battle of Berlin in the winter of 1943–44, and morale in some squadrons was not at its best. Although there were on average 594 Lancasters available for operations in 1944, production was only narrowly exceeding losses and the re-equipment of No. 3 Group with the Lancaster was proceeding slowly: in March 1944, four of the Group's squadrons were still flying a dwindling number of the obsolete Short Stirling B.III. These squadrons had been withdrawn from raids over Germany in November 1943 but would take part in the raids across France during the spring of 1944.

The withdrawal of the Stirling left the Handley Page Halifax, inferior to the Lancaster in speed and ceiling, as the aircraft most vulnerable to flak and fighters. In consequence, the Halifax became the subject of increasing criticism by the Bomber Command hierarchy in late 1943. The Halifax B.II and B.V were withdrawn from operations over Germany after the Leipzig raid on 19–20 February 1944, in which 34 Halifaxes (13.3 per cent of those deployed) were lost. The Bristol Hercules-powered Halifax B.III, which began to enter squadrons in substantial numbers in February 1944, did close the performance gap to the Lancaster to a large extent. Yet even the B.III never found real favour with Portal and Harris, who continued to press for its replacement with the Lancaster. In early 1944, the Halifax equipped No. 4 Group and most of the Canadian No. 6 Group, both based in Yorkshire. By March 1944, morale in No. 4 Group was uncertain, and it is no coincidence that the Group's commander was visiting squadrons on the subject of early returns.

The Pathfinder Force

In early 1944, 8 Group (the Pathfinder Force, or PFF), based in Cambridgeshire, comprised six Lancaster and four de Havilland Mosquito squadrons. The Mosquito pathfinder crews were generally drawn from those who had completed a tour on Main Force squadrons: most Mosquito pilots had over 1,000 hours' experience and they were considered the 'old men' of Bomber Command. Under the dynamic leadership of Air Vice Marshal Donald Bennett, the PFF had enjoyed a series of successes across 1943. Unfortunately, his command had been sorely tried by heavy losses in the winter campaign. The Official History commented that by early 1944, 8 Group had to manage with 'a dead weight' of ex-Operational Training Unit crews (new crews with little experience), and it is certain that in March 1944, neither experience nor competence in 8 Group were at the standard Bennett demanded.

The formidable Australian, Air Vice Marshal Don Bennett, commanded Bomber Command's Pathfinder Force during the campaign. His Group had developed tactics for large-scale area bombing raids on city centres, but as more precise attacks became necessary, his position began to be undermined by the successes achieved by No. 5 Group. (Alamy Stock Photo)

Equipment and tactics

Since the war's beginning, RAF Bomber Command had made enormous strides – mainly in the form of much-enhanced destructive power. At the same time, there were still two principal difficulties. The most important from the crews' point of view was survivability, while from the point of view of the populations of France and Belgium the most important was bombing accuracy. Reducing the number of bombers lost to flak or fighters and improving bombing accuracy were 'force multipliers'. Much time and thought was given to both problems.

Two basic factors would serve to help these objectives. The first was the shorter distances involved. Then there was the possibility of improved weather conditions as spring approached. The crews of Bomber Command could reasonably expect the forthcoming campaign to be, if not a series of 'milk runs', then substantially easier to survive than the long flights into Germany. With the possibility of (relatively) limited night-fighter opposition, there was an opportunity to increase accuracy by mounting operations on moonlit nights.

In the coming campaign, Bomber Command would deploy Oboe, a blind-bombing device used by the Pathfinder Force's Mosquitoes to excellent effect. Oboe's accuracy is difficult to determine: the Official History wisely stated that it could be measured in terms of hundreds of yards. Another blind-bombing aid, H2S, was a ground-mapping radar installed in the heavy bombers. The device was afflicted by a number of shortcomings, but worked best when delineating the difference between land and water. The results H2S offered were decidedly mixed and Bomber Command was fortunate that most targets in France were within Oboe range, about 270 miles from the East Coast of the UK.

In clear visibility – a relatively rare occurrence – some form of visual target marking could be used. In cloudy conditions, the aiming point was marked using Oboe or H2S. Pathfinders dropped Target Indicators, or 'sky markers' suspended from parachutes. The latter naturally drifted with the wind and only remained visible until they disappeared below the clouds. Subsequent re-marking with sky markers by PFF 'backers-up' compounded the problem of drift, resulting in poor bombing accuracy.

The late winter of 1943–44 generally involved high-altitude blind marking for area attacks. Faced with increasing calls during the early stages of the Transportation Plan campaign for precision attacks, Harris encouraged the individual Groups to explore alternative marking methods. Ralph Cochrane's No. 5 Group was considered by many as the crème de la crème of Bomber Command. The Group, which included the elite 617 Squadron, developed tactics for precision attacks, quickly becoming a serious rival to Bennett's pathfinders.

It was well known that the better defended the target, the less accurate the bombing. One phenomenon of this was 'creep back', in which bombing progressively 'crept back' as successive crews bombed short of the visible fires. The majority of bombs dropped by Bomber

The austere features of No. 5 Group's commander, Air Vice Marshal the Hon Ralph Cochrane. More than most Group commanders, Cochrane strongly pressed for improvements in bombing accuracy. No. 5 Group attracted a measure of jealousy, but there is no doubt that morale and bombing performance were the best in Bomber Command. (Crown Copyright, MoD)

The first of Bomber Command's trio of heavy bombers, the Short Stirling had reached the end of the road by late 1943. In truth, the type had become obsolete the previous year. The remaining four squadrons in No. 3 Group continued to fly minelaying sorties, as well as short-distance sorties against French targets. (Imperial War Museums, HU 62974)

Commanding the Eighth Air Force in the spring of 1944, the dynamic General James (Jimmy) Doolittle shared Spaatz's vision for a decisive contribution by the American bomber fleets in Europe. Although heavy losses were incurred between February and May 1944, the Luftwaffe was defeated. (US Army Signal Corps/Interim Archives/Getty Images)

Command over railway centres in 1944 were high explosive. Incendiary bombs, successful in fire-raising in city centres, were considered less effective. A German survey in late 1944 discovered that 18.9 per cent of RAF bombs failed to explode, against 12.2 per cent of those dropped by the USAAF.

Therefore, on the eve of the campaign, in late February 1944, Bomber Command represented something of a curate's egg in terms of experience, capability and morale. Some of the heaviest losses of the war, notably over Berlin and Nuremberg, still lay in the future. For all that, Bomber Command was able, given the right conditions, to drop vast quantities of high explosive and incendiary bombs and to lay waste to large towns in a single night.

The United States Strategic Air Forces

The Pointblank directive of May 1943 applied equally to RAF Bomber Command and the US Eighth Air Force. Nonetheless, while the two air fleets shared the same broad objectives, in reality their respective campaigns were fought more or less independently. For the Eighth Air Force, the important part of the directive was the identification of those target systems vital to the Reich's war economy (mainly the German aircraft industry, ball bearing manufacture, oil and synthetic rubber production). In the directive's words, the 'destruction and dislocation' of these would 'gravely impair and might paralyze the western Axis war effort'. Overriding this was the 'Intermediate Objective', 'a prior (or simultaneous) offensive against the German fighter strength'. 'To carry out the Eighth Air Force's part of this combined bomber offensive,' the directive added, 'it will be necessary to attack precision targets deep in German territory in daylight.'

In accordance with these instructions, the Eighth Air Force had battled ever further into Germany in 1943, fighting a series of increasingly bloody encounters with the Luftwaffe as it did so. These missions culminated with the loss of 60 bombers in each of the two attacks on ball bearing production in Schweinfurt in August and October 1943. These losses were unsustainable. In early January 1944, statistics showed that 74 per cent of crews would not complete the standard 'tour' of 25 missions. Of these, 57 per cent would be dead or missing. Unsurprisingly, morale suffered.

In late December 1943, General Ira Eaker was replaced as head of the Eighth Air Force by General James Doolittle, a more thrusting commander who was determined to seek and destroy the Luftwaffe at every opportunity. The crucial turning point came with the supply of longer-range drop tanks for the P-47 escort fighters, together with the introduction of the P-51. In late February 1944, the Eighth and Fifteenth Air Forces launched Operation *Argument*, striking over and again at the German aircraft industry. More importantly, it began the grim battle of attrition which would plunge the defence of the Reich into a vicious circle of spiralling losses.

Compounding the Luftwaffe's issues was the formation in November 1943 of the Fifteenth Air Force, based in Italy. In February 1944, the Fifteenth fielded 12 heavy Bombardment Groups but would play only a minor role in the preparations for *Overlord*.

Aircraft

By 1944, the Boeing B-17 Flying Fortress was a relatively old design. The B-17F, which had been at the forefront of the serious losses in the summer and autumn campaign of 1943, began to be replaced by the B-17G in September 1943. The lessons provided by the Luftwaffe's frontal attacks were addressed by the provision of two .50cal machine guns in the new model's remote-controlled Bendix chin turret. The 'Fort' equipped two of the three Eighth Air Force's Bombardment Divisions.

Boeing B-17G Flying Fortresses, 381st Bomb Group, Eighth Air Force, mid-1944. Some missions were flown against transportation targets, especially those in western Germany. However, Spaatz and Doolittle preferred to send the bombers and escorting fighters against the Reich's synthetic oil refineries, forcing the Jagdwaffe into costly air battles with the American air armadas. (Universal History Archive/UIG/Getty Images)

The Consolidated B-24 Liberator formed the equipment of the Eighth's Second Bombardment Division. The 'Lib', with its carefully designed 'Davis wing', represented a generational shift from the B-17, to which it was superior in speed and range. However, relatively sleepy handling, which made tight formation-keeping difficult, and a perceived tendency to catch fire easily did not endear the B-24 to some crews. The B-24G and H models introduced a powered nose turret intended, like that of the B-17G, to increase the forward firepower of the American formations.

Precision bombing?

The USAAF doctrine of precision bombing relied to a large extent on the fabled Norden gyroscope-stabilised bombsight. Asked if bombardiers really could drop a bomb down a pickle barrel from 20,000ft, the bombsight's designer, Carl Norden, is alleged to have replied, 'Which pickle do you want to hit?' The Norden did indeed give good results (an average error of about 300yds) in ideal conditions, but the reality in North-West Europe was different. Under combat conditions, the error could be five times greater and the 'circular error probable' for Eighth Air Force visual bombing over the whole war was about three-quarters of a mile.

On average, poor weather prevented the Eighth Air Force flying on about 25 per cent of days. The Eighth responded by forming a pathfinder unit, the 482nd Bomb Group. The 482nd's aircraft, equipped with H2X, an American development of H2S, took the lead in attacks on targets obscured by cloud. Throughout the war, the Eighth bombed

B-24 Liberators of the 458th Bomb Group, with their Mustang escort. The B-24 Groups of the 2nd Air Division participated alongside the B-17 Groups in the attacks made after 1 May against communication targets on either side of the French–German border. (PhotoQuest/Getty Images)

The crew of the *Question Mark*, 1929. From left, Roy Hooe, Elwood Quesada, Henry Halverson, Ira Eaker and Carl Spaatz. (Associated Press/Alamy Stock Photo)

French *resisteurs* sabotage a section of line. The Allies thought the activities of the Resistance, while valuable, were haphazard and uncoordinated. SNCF sources, on the other hand, wanted a fuller Resistance campaign instead of Allied bombing with its effects on the surrounding areas. (Photo12/Alamy Stock Photo)

visually only about 50 per cent of the time, and in the winter of 1943–44, after Arnold sanctioned radar bombing, it was only 10 per cent. Results were similar to those achieved by Bomber Command's H2S-led efforts: bombing within a mile of the aiming point was considered a good result. Crews called it 'blind bombing', but, publicly at least, it was referred to as 'bombing through overcast'. Some historians have criticised the hypocrisy of the American avowal of 'precision bombing' versus the reality of their campaign. Yet, the *intention* of the USSTAF was always different to that of the area bombing policy of Bomber Command, even if the effect was often indistinguishable to those on the receiving end. Moreover, blind bombing did enable the USSTAF to fly missions on days when poor weather would otherwise have 'scrubbed' operations.

In the late winter of 1943–44, the fortunes of the Eighth Air Force and Bomber Command were waxing and waning in equal proportion. Harris remained keen to pursue the area bombing campaign, even in the face of growing dissatisfaction among the Chiefs of Staff and the Air Ministry. Spaatz and Doolittle felt that the battle for daylight air superiority was approaching the crisis point; the crippling of the German war economy should surely follow. At the same time, a good deal of discord surrounded the command of these substantial forces, as well as the operational and political ramifications of their pre-*Overlord* deployment.

The Resistance

Finally, although it cannot properly be considered part of the forthcoming campaign, brief mention should be made of the Resistance in Occupied Europe. The Resistance was not a single entity but a highly complex and loose-structured organization, deeply divided both politically and regionally. At its head, presiding over the French Committee of National Liberation, stood the imposing figure of General Charles de Gaulle, together with his UK-based subordinate and SHAEF representative, General Pierre-Joseph Koenig. Allied operational liaison with the Resistance was through the British Special Operations Executive (SOE) and the American OSS. The Allied agencies channelled funds, weaponry and supplies to the Resistance, as well as agents, in an attempt to provide a measure of co-ordination to its activities. The Resistance's main value consisted of sending a mass of information to London concerning the German defensive measures. Passive resistance, notably railway strikes and go-slows, did a great deal of harm to the transport infrastructure. As the invasion approached, more direct action would be undertaken.

The Messerschmitt Me 110G was one of the two *Nachtjäger* which constituted the main threat to Bomber Command in the early months of 1944. This example, interned in Switzerland, was equipped with the aerials for the then-new Lichtenstein SN-2 long-range radar and the earlier shorter-range Lichtenstein C-1 radar. (Imperial War Museums, HU 108218)

DEFENDER'S CAPABILITIES

Since 1941, the fighting in Russia and the Mediterranean had steadily drained army and Luftwaffe units away from the West. By the spring of 1944, the German air and land defences in France had suffered from almost three years of relative neglect. Then over the course of 1943, the increasing weight of the Allied Pointblank offensive had forced the Luftwaffe to concentrate much of its day fighter strength within Germany. This chapter will examine the target of the Allied air forces, the French and Belgian railways, before considering the active and passive measures in place for their defence.

The Allied bombing of France to 1944

In June 1940, France was divided into two zones. In the north and west, the Germans occupied the important ports and industrial centres. The greater part of the country was an 'unoccupied zone', controlled by the Vichy government. RAF guidelines, governing the bombing of French targets, were issued in 1940, and again in October 1942. Both stressed the need for caution.

In 1942, Bomber Command was directed to assist in the Battle of the Atlantic by attacking France's west-coast U-boat bases; the violent but ineffective offensive against the French ports was eventually halted in April 1943. Meanwhile, the Eighth Air Force had been bombing French targets since August 1942. In these, high-altitude and inexperienced crews combined to (unintentionally) scatter bombs over urban areas, to the anger of the population.

Although raids on France were reduced in mid-1943, the Eighth returned to France in August and September, targeting the aircraft industry in accordance with the Pointblank directive. By the end of 1943, the French civilian death toll for the year from Allied bombing was 7,458, nearly three times that of 1942. A French report which reached London in early 1944 highlighted the bombing on a people 'tired, worn out by all its miseries … [and] unnerved by too long a wait for liberation'. An unflattering testament to Bomber Command's inaccuracy was provided by a 1943 *Armée de l'Air* report on the results of raids on Paris and

Montluçon. The writers, puzzled by the wide scatter of bombs, were unable to understand the primary purpose of the attacks. Similarly, contemporary French calculations showed that Allied raids during 1943 and early 1944 covered an average area of 2–4km^2.

A contrast, albeit only partial, was provided by the use of fighter-bombers over France. The relative accuracy shown by the RAF and USAAF tactical squadrons was applauded by some in France. On the other hand, the practice of strafing and bombing French trains became a definite source of contention. Many rural French communities relied on the railways for even the most basic necessities, including food produce, coal and commuting. The disregard shown by Allied pilots, many of whom regarded train strafing as something of a 'lark', began to have a serious effect as the war went on.

Passive resistance, or anything open to interpretation as such, carried its own risks. Refusal to take up a civil defence post or failure to observe the blackout could be identified by the Germans as an act of resistance, with its own severe penalties. The slow introduction of French anti-aircraft units in the summer of 1943 was blamed by the Germans on a network of Freemasons among the French officials involved. Most tellingly, the death penalty was introduced in 1941 for any French civilians found to be helping Allied airmen evade capture.

The target: The French railway network

France's railway lines radiate from Paris like the spokes in a wheel. These lines connect the towns and cities in the provinces and the ports in the north and west, and join up with the Belgian and German networks in the east. Paris itself is encircled by the important *Grande Ceinture*, which links the lines emanating from the capital. Clustered around Paris and the major towns and ports are a profusion of railway centres: the locomotive depots and marshalling yards instrumental in the running of the system.

The 'Convention of 1859' gave each of the major French railway companies a virtual monopoly in its region. The result, unlike in Britain, was that there was no 'railway craze', with duplicated lines in competition with one another. Some argued that this made it a tempting target for air attack. The French government nationalised France's railways in 1938, forming the SNCF (*Société nationale des chemins de fer français*). The SNCF had been in

The Villeneuve St Georges rail centre, *circa* 1936. Villeneuve was the main Paris yard for *Region Sud* and this view shows the vast extent of the typical Parisian rail centres. Disabling the facilities of the main centres required the hitting power of the RAF and USAAF heavy bombers. (Keystone-France/Gamma-Rapho via Getty Images)

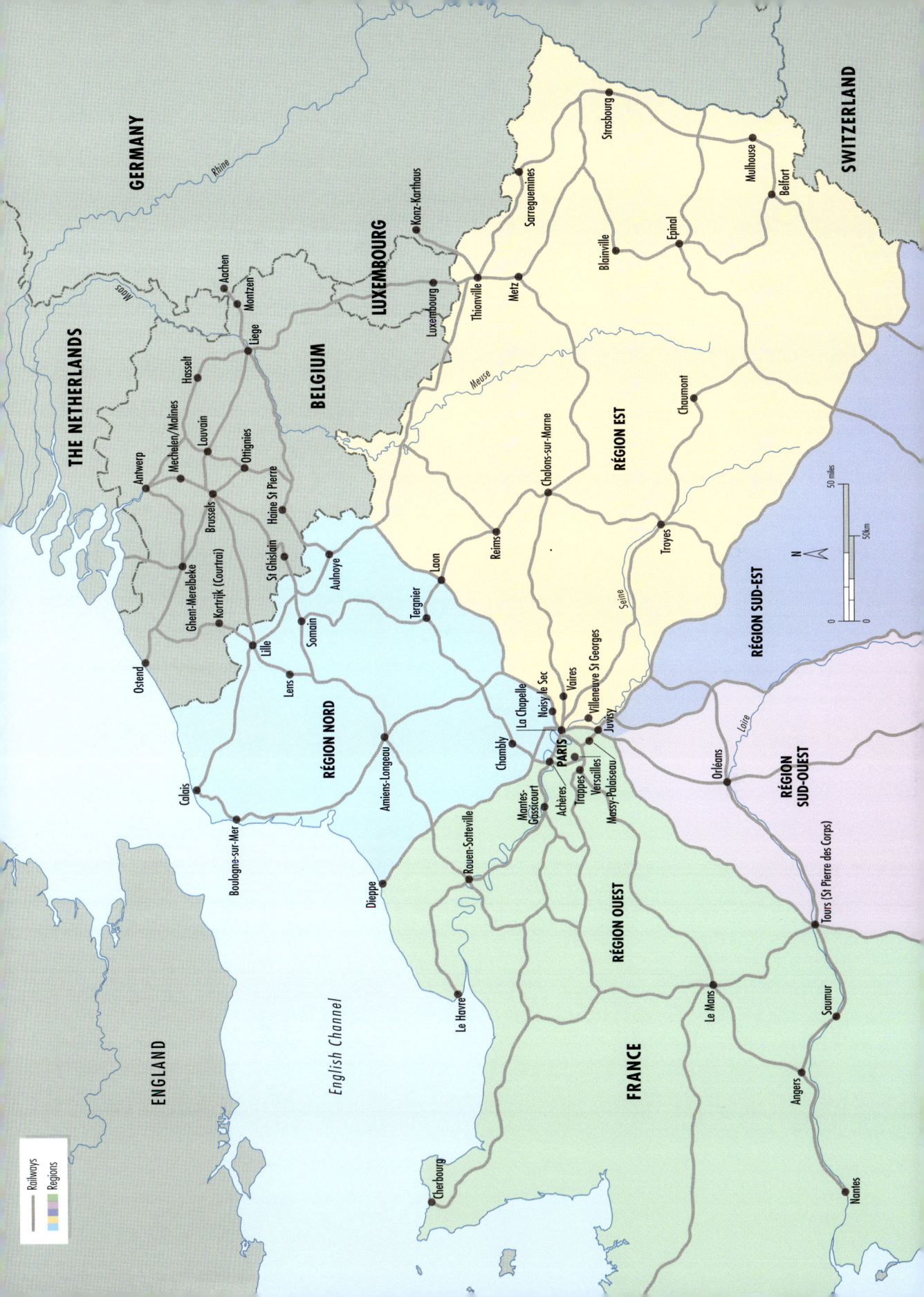

existence for just six years by 1944, and was still struggling to integrate the pre-nationalisation regions into a unified whole. Idiosyncrasies in equipment were yet to be overcome, as well as the different methods and attitudes which marked the personnel of the five regions. The SNCF regions – the *Nord, Est, Sud-Est, Sud-Ouest* and *Ouest* – essentially paralleled the pre-nationalisation railway companies.

About 66 per cent of traffic on the French system was devoted to passenger services and the rest to freight. It was therefore apparent that a large percentage of the overall traffic could be eliminated without danger to the national economy. The *Nord* and *Est* regions, which served the industrial areas of north-eastern France, carried the lion's share of freight. There were some electrified lines, mostly in *Region Sud-Ouest*. In 1938, the SNCF employed 500,000 staff and owned 18,000 locomotives, 31,000 coaches and 480,000 goods wagons and vans.

After the armistice in 1940, the SNCF had a curious, and at times chaotic, accumulation of German authorities forcibly imposed upon it. In brief, these were three overlapping organizations:

- Military transport was the responsibility of *General des Transportwesens West* (General of Transportation West), headquartered in Paris.
- German economic and military traffic was the responsibility of the *Hauptverkehrsdirektion* (HVD, Main Traffic Directorate), which had two headquarters: one in Paris for *Region Nord* and another, based in Brussels, for *Region Est*.
- The *Gebietsverkehrsleitung West* (Area Traffic Management West) managed traffic between Germany and France.

The German state railway, the *Deutsche Reichsbahn*, ruthlessly plundered the French railways after the armistice. By 1944, the SNCF had 'loaned' to Germany 30 per cent of its locomotives and 35 per cent of its rolling stock, while unknown but considerable quantities of materiel had been appropriated. Around 80 per cent of traffic consisted of German trains. The personnel working on the French railways had been reduced by 20 per cent. A severe reduction in turnaround times (loading and unloading) was instituted through a variety of measures in a bid to maximise the capacity of the freight system. Locomotives and rolling stock were required to work harder for longer, yet routine maintenance was drastically cut down or omitted altogether.

Efficient railway networks rely on the methodical planning of rail movements. By 1944, the French network, despite being part of a larger pan-European system, was under-maintained, overburdened and suffering from Franco-German antagonism in its administration. Some Allied planners and rail experts hoped that this illogical and unrealistic organization would struggle to cope with a series of severe and unpredictable interferences.

The active defences: fighters and flak

The Luftwaffe defence of France, Belgium and the Netherlands was the responsibility of Luftflotte 3, commanded by Generalfeldmarschall Hugo Sperrle. An infantry officer, Sperrle transferred to the Luftwaffe in 1935 and had commanded Luftflotte 3 during the Battles of France and Britain and then the Blitz campaign of 1940–41. Sperrle was noted less for his military acumen than for his considerable organizational skills; he was known above all for his abrasive personality. By 1944, Luftflotte 3 had become something of a poor relation within the Luftwaffe, and the passive leadership displayed by Sperrle reflected this.

However, incursions into eastern French and Belgian airspace could be contested by Luftflotte Reich, responsible for the air defence of Germany itself. By early 1944, Luftflotte Reich boasted several formidable night-fighter units and an even larger number of day fighter units, which had largely been drawn from the Eastern and Italian fronts over the course of 1943. Complex plans existed for Luftflotte 3's reinforcement by Luftflotte Reich in the event of the expected Allied invasion.

By the early spring of 1944, pilot training was cut back to around 150 hours in order to meet higher losses. This compared with the 400 hours received by American pilots. The result was a chaotic and lethal mix of high-powered aircraft and young, undertrained Luftwaffe pilots. In the first six months of 1944, 1,345 fighters were lost in non-combat-related incidents.

The day fighters

At the end of March 1944, Luftflotte 3 could call on just two fighter groups, Jagdgeschwader (JG) 2 and JG 26, with a combined operational strength of 32 Messerschmitt Me 109s and 83 Focke-Wulf Fw 190s. In 1944, the Me 109G was the standard equipment of all the Luftwaffe's remaining Messerschmitt units, but was outclassed by most of the Allied fighters it faced. Although superior in most respects to its Messerschmitt stablemate, by 1944 the Fw 190 had lost the advantage previously enjoyed over its Allied rivals. When new large-capacity drop tanks, and the P-51 Mustang, became available to the USAAF in early 1944, the German fighters turned from the hunters to the hunted. The main objective of Luftflotte 3's fighters was to conserve strength for the invasion – even if this meant avoiding combat with the well-armed and heavily escorted American bombers over France.

Panther tanks *en route* to Normandy. The tanks of the German panzer divisions in France were unsuitable for long-distance road travel, and the reinforcement of the battle area by the powerful armoured counter-attack reserve therefore depended on fast and efficient rail movement. (ullstein bild via Getty Images)

The night fighters

In contrast to the declining fortunes of the day fighters, the Luftwaffe's *Nachtjagdgruppen* (night-fighter groups) were enjoying growing success over the first months of 1944. Luftflotte 3's night-fighter units – NJG 4, together with elements of NJG 5 and 6 – were fewer in number and had seen less action than their comrades based in Germany. Nevertheless, they were able to inflict major losses on Bomber Command as the pre-invasion campaign developed.

Luftflotte 3's night-fighter units were equipped almost entirely with the Messerschmitt Me 110. This extraordinarily successful night fighter offered a heavy armament, superb handling and good endurance. It became the mount of many of the leading Luftwaffe night-fighter aces. The Me 110's main rival was the Ju 88. Larger and heavier, the Ju 88 gradually superseded the Me 110 over the last two years of the war, although it never replaced the latter completely.

Two key developments were central to the success of both types during the winter of 1943–44. The first was the introduction of new electronic equipment. The *Flensburg* receiver homed onto the transmissions of Bomber Command's Monica tail-warning radar. Similarly, *Naxos* detected the emissions produced by the H2S ground-mapping radar, although the success claimed is probably exaggerated. Finally, the Lichtenstein SN-2 airborne radar entered service in late 1943. This operated on a frequency not yet jammed by 'Window' (thin metallic strips dropped in their thousands that confused German radar operators). By May 1944, over 1,000 Lichtenstein sets had been delivered. The second development was the fitting of two 30mm cannon at an angle behind the cockpit of an Me 110 or Ju 88. This, the famous *schräge musik* (the colloquial German translation of 'jazz music'), was introduced in mid-1943 and allowed the night fighters to approach and attack their victims unseen from below. It immediately proved devastatingly effective.

Flak

Static flak defences in France were concentrated around important targets such as airfields, rail centres and factory complexes. The basic flak unit was the battery, usually with four to eight guns apiece. The Luftwaffe operated heavy flak batteries (most of which were equipped with the famous 88mm gun), light and mixed flak units, and searchlights. There was also the *Eisenbahnflak*, a mobile reserve of heavy and light flak trains. During 1942, in response to American daylight bombing and the RAF's bomber streams, the Luftwaffe began to form *Grossbatterien* (Grand batteries). These grouped together heavy batteries of the same gun calibre, which fired from a joint command post. The number of heavy batteries in the West doubled between 1943 and 1944, in anticipation of an Allied landing.

A good deal had been written on the effectiveness or otherwise of German flak. In 1944, 16,000 88mm shells were fired for every bomber shot down. This reflects a serious decline in flak performance during that year, which was attributable to two factors. The increase in shells fired wore out gun barrels faster, and these struggled to engage the high-flying American day bombers. Worn barrels also carried a risk of exploding: in 1944, 380 Flak 88s were lost through excessive wear or destruction, twice the equivalent figure for 1943. This was allied to a decline in the quality of flak crews, for the ranks of the flak arm were continually combed through to address an ever-worsening manpower crisis in the army. The recruitment of French anti-aircraft crews offered only a partial solution, for the adherence of these crews to their duty remained doubtful.

Light and medium flak

In 1944, there were two basic medium flak guns in service. The 37mm Flak 36 could fire 80 rounds per minute, while the improved 37mm Flak 43 doubled the rate of fire to 160 rounds per minute. Their effective ceiling was 5,000ft. The 37mm guns were usually deployed in concentrations of between nine and 12 guns. These were very powerful indeed, with a single hit able to bring down a large Allied fighter-bomber such as the P-47. The lighter 20mm Flak 38 was usually deployed in concentrations of 12–15 guns. The effective ceiling was 3,500ft and the maximum rate of fire was 700–800 rounds per minute.

A battery of formidable 88mm flak guns fire into the night sky. The decline of the Luftwaffe's fighters shifted the onus of air defence in France onto the flak arm. Shortages of ammunition, inadequately trained crews and poor accuracy meant that flak was not the deterrent it should have been. (ullstein bild via Getty Images)

Light and medium flak was concentrated in areas vulnerable to medium bombers and fighter-bombers, such as railway centres and bridges. Both 37mm and 20mm guns were installed as standard on railway flatcars, where they were often the first target for Allied pilots once the locomotive had been rendered immobile. In 1944, there were 837 flak batteries of all types in France, Belgium and the Netherlands, 20 per cent of Germany's available total.

Passive defence measures

The weakness of the German fighter and flak defences in northern France shifted the onus of responsibility onto passive defensive measures, which included an air raid warning system, bomb shelters and organizations which cared for and rehoused those who had lost their homes.

Like many states, France had begun to seriously plan its civil defence in the mid-1930s. After the surrender in June 1940, however, civil defence fragmented. Towns in the unoccupied, Vichy-controlled zone were rarely attacked and the issue of civil defence from 1940 to late 1942 became clouded by a degree of apathy. On the other hand, although towns in the German zone were more likely to be bombed, the Germans made sure that the flak defences available were concentrated around key assets: airfields, ports and factory complexes.

In February 1943, in response to the spread of Allied bombing into the former unoccupied zone (controlled by the Nazis since November 1942), the German authorities ordered the establishment of a new unified system for active and passive defence. New anti-aircraft batteries were formed, initially under the control of the army, before the Luftwaffe took them back. A new air raid warning system, the *Securité Aérienne Publique* (Public Air Safety), was activated, under *Armée de l'Air* control. It relied on air raid alerts from French officials being passed to their German superiors, with the result that warnings were often sounded too late.

Evacuation was the pre-war French government's preferred solution to civil defence, but after 1940, the emphasis was changed to stop people leaving prematurely. In February 1944, the Nazi-controlled French government again favoured evacuation, giving priority to children, mothers and the elderly. It is estimated that about 1.2 million people consented to evacuation, although, as in Britain, many did so reluctantly.

The government did its best to make political capital from the Allied attacks. Large and elaborate funerals with plentiful media coverage were staged. Vichy-controlled newspapers likewise did their best to stir up anti-British and American feeling. After three-and-a-half years, popular goodwill towards the RAF and USAAF began to decline. BBC broadcasts tried to portray bombing and liberation as two sides of the same coin. Propaganda and warning leaflets were dropped in great profusion and France was deluged by a shower of paper. From March 1944, a million leaflets a month were dropped until D-Day. It was difficult for the French to know how to respond to the raids. They were not at war. They wanted the Allies who were bombing them to win and the Germans who 'protected' them to lose. Yet it was the Allies who were killing them, if only in order to bring about the long-awaited day of liberation.

The Prussian hauteur of Feldmarschall Gerd von Rundstedt. By 1944, Rundstedt, commanding German armies in the West, was old, war-weary and preferred to delegate the day-to-day issues afflicting the Wehrmacht in France to his subordinates – including the disposition of the valuable armoured divisions. (Heinrich Hoffmann/ullstein bild via Getty Images)

The German Army in the West

The transfer of German Army units from west to east was reversed in November 1943 by Hitler's Directive No. 51, which anticipated an Allied landing in Europe the following year. By June 1944, there were almost 70 infantry and armoured divisions in France, Belgium and the Netherlands, but the quality of these units varied considerably in terms of training, experience, equipment, mobility and morale.

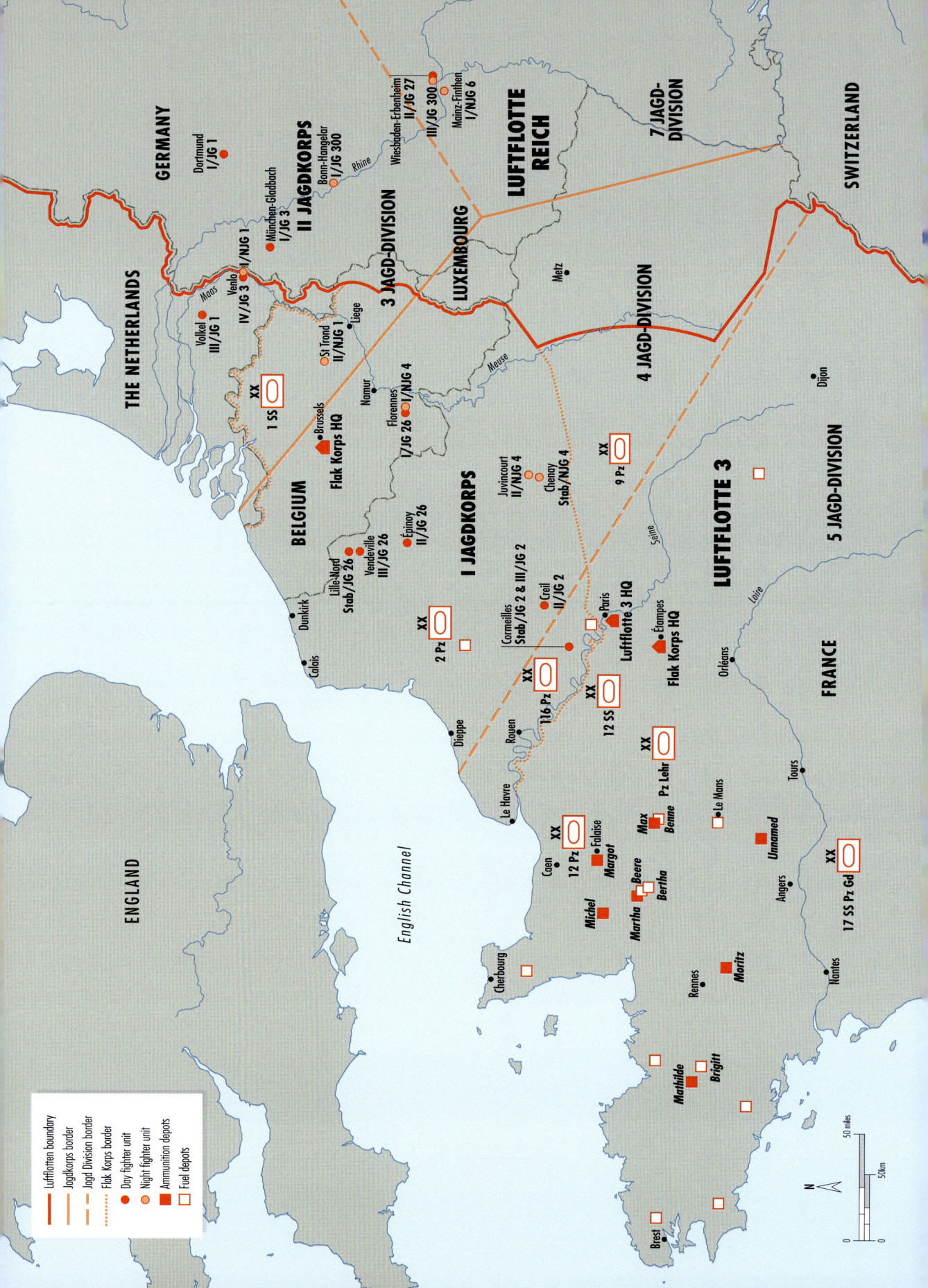

OPPOSITE THE GERMAN DEFENCES: WEST: MARCH–JUNE 1944

At the head of the German chain of command in the West was the Fuhrer, Adolf Hitler. Next came Supreme Commander West, the elderly Feldmarschall Gerd von Rundstedt. Under Rundstedt were two Army Groups. Army Group G was located south of the Loire, while Army Group B was in the north, commanded by Feldmarschall Erwin Rommel. Army Group B comprised two armies: the Seventh Army covered the north-west of France, including Normandy; the Fifteenth Army held the north-east. Army Group B possessed the majority of infantry divisions, although some, intended only to hold coastal defences, were of doubtful value.

The jewel in the crown was the armoured reserve of nine panzer, and one panzer-grenadier, divisions. Another two armoured divisions on the Eastern Front were earmarked for transfer when the invasion came. In brief, these divisions were:

German Panzer Divisions for the defence of the West, June 1944			
Panzer Division	Location	Allocation	Notes
2nd Panzer	Around Amiens	Army Group B	War-weary but up to strength
21st Panzer	Normandy	Army Group B	Close to full-strength
116th Panzer	South-east of Rouen	Army Group B	Partially trained and lacking transport
12th SS Panzer	Near Normandy	I SS Panzerkorps	Understrength
Panzer Lehr	Near Le Mans	I SS Panzerkorps	Well-trained and equipped
9th Panzer	Mailly-le-Camp	Panzer Group West	Understrength
1st SS Panzer	North-east of Brussels	Panzer Group West	War-weary
2nd SS Panzer	North-east of Toulouse	Panzer Group West	War-weary and lacking transport
17th SS Panzer-Grenadier	South-west of Tours	Panzer Group West	Not combat-ready and lacking transport
9th SS Panzer	Eastern Front	To be allocated	Lacking transport
10th SS Panzer	Eastern Front	To be allocated	Understrength

Their potential was reduced by disagreement over the way they should be deployed. Until he was certain of the main Allied invasion, Hitler determined to keep in reserve six armoured divisions. Only once the panzers were concentrated would a powerful armoured counterattack be launched. Rommel, with his experience of Allied air power, knew that the invasion had to be pushed back into the sea as soon as possible. The result was a compromise. Rommel was allocated the 2nd, 21st and 116th Panzer Divisions. These were based near the coast to meet an Allied landing, but in themselves were unlikely to be strong enough to be decisive. The I SS Panzerkorps controlled the 12th SS and Panzer Lehr Divisions, while the remaining four divisions (1st and 2nd SS Panzer and the 9th and 10th Panzer) were allocated to Panzer Group West. All six divisions of this powerful reserve were scattered across France. 'This dispersal of strength,' wrote Germany's armour expert, Heinz Guderian, 'ruled out all possibility of a great defensive victory.' Unless, that is, the Germans could make use of their customary power of manoeuvre.

The logistical situation

Since the middle of 1943, the Wehrmacht had been progressively 'de-motorised' through attrition and fuel shortages. Between 1 February and 1 May 1944, the German Army's deficit in trucks and prime movers increased by 127 per cent and 46 per cent respectively. Before D-Day, the Seventh Army had only 1,035 million tons of fuel, or enough for about two weeks of mobile operations. The mobile reserves had enough fuel for seven to ten days of operations.

About 90 per cent of the German Army therefore relied on marching, horse-drawn transport and the railways, especially in the case of the panzer divisions based in France. For infantry divisions, the minimum limit for rail movement was 120km. On average, an infantry division could march the same distance in three days, whereas the average equivalent rail journey would take eight days. The German policy for the movement of reinforcing units was for no armoured division to move less than 300km by rail – any shorter distance made the process of marshalling and loading and unloading of the necessary trains uneconomic. With this in mind, three measures were implemented to minimise road and rail disruption before D-Day:

Feldmarschall Erwin Rommel, commander of Army Group B, seen on one of his many inspections of the Atlantic Wall. Rommel maintained painful memories of Allied air superiority in North Africa and therefore wanted the panzer divisions able to move to the beachhead as quickly as possible. (AFP via Getty Images)

1. Military and civilian trucks began to be rigorously confiscated. Attempts to remedy the insufficiency of motor transport in the months before *Overlord* were compromised by low vehicle production and an increase in demand caused by the arrival of worn-out divisions from the East and the creation of new units in France. In January 1944, exercises showed that without the French railways, the army would require 40,000 tons of trucking capacity to counter an Allied landing – more than eight times the available strategic transport reserve. On the eve of D-Day, the Seventh Army possessed 18,748 tons of stockpiled munitions, enough for about three weeks of combat. Of this, only 7,172 tons (38 per cent) was in Normandy, the rest being in Brittany. Further supplies relied on deliveries from the major reserve depots around Paris, and this, as with so much of the German Army's logistical requirements, would depend overwhelmingly on a sound rail network.
2. Anti-aircraft batteries were moved to important rail centres and bridges.
3. Rail engineer and bridge-building units were strengthened and redeployed to the Seine. (In spring 1944, there was only one regiment of railway engineers in the West.) Nine repair trains were readied and hidden around the network in obscure sidings. When a coded signal – 'Hannibal' – was received, the nearest repair train was sent to the damaged rail centre or bridge, which was usually reached within five or six hours. Four of the repair trains were specifically designed for bridge-rebuilding and each train could deal with 60m of destroyed bridge. Of the rest, two specialized in railway line cuts and three repaired signal installations and communications. Supplies of spares and equipment were located at depots in Rennes, Reims and Dijon. Enough coal for two weeks of continuous rail movement was stockpiled.

CAMPAIGN OBJECTIVES

The pre-*Overlord* air plan eventually adopted did not emerge without a good deal of argument, and more than a little acrimony. Throughout the period between late December 1943 and early March 1944, there were three main issues at stake. These were, in the order in which they surfaced: the problem of command, the question of which pre-*Overlord* plan to adopt and the political concerns over excessive French civilian casualties. These matters intertwined with one another to produce a complex picture in which the individual threads are separated only with difficulty. These issues were to form the battle lines in debates over the campaign's effectiveness in the months and years to come.

For Eisenhower, the overriding priority was the firm establishment of a lodgement in Normandy. This meant building up a force sufficient to meet a probable German counterattack, after which a breakout into France could be made. Much, therefore, depended on the respective rates of Allied and German build-up in Normandy, which were expected by SHAEF to be more or less equal.

Much depended on the skill of the Oboe-equipped Mosquito pathfinder squadrons. The Mosquito's high performance conferred a long service career on some, and the crew of Mosquito B. IX, LR 503, of No. 105 Squadron is celebrating the aircraft's 203rd sortie. This Mosquito eventually completed a remarkable 213 missions. (Crown Copyright, MoD)

Estimates of respective rates of build-up, 1943 and May 1944				
	COSSAC's original estimate of German build-up, 1943	COSSAC's original estimate of Allied build-up, 1943	Revised estimate of German build-up, SHAEF, May 1944	Revised estimate of Allied build-up, SHAEF, May 1944
D-Day	3	5.66	3	8.66
D+2	5	9.5	6–7	10.5
D+8	9	14.66	11–14	15.66

Zuckerman's plan

When Arthur Tedder and Solly Zuckerman returned to the UK at the end of 1943, they found a pre-*Overlord* plan for the air forces already existed, 'Neptune Study No. 6, Delay of Enemy Reserves'. This had been drawn up by the COSSAC/AEAF Joint Planning Staff, with

Wrecked rolling stock in the marshalling yard in Catania, Sicily, August 1943. Solly Zuckerman's Transportation Plan for France and Belgium owed much to the campaign against Sicilian and southern Italian rail centres in 1943. Others thought that Zuckerman had drawn the wrong conclusions from the earlier campaigns. (Associated Press/Alamy Stock Photo)

much input from Brant and Sherrington, the two experts at the Railway Research Service. The plan proposed bombing 17 rail centres in an arc some 50–60 miles from the chosen area in Normandy. On account of security, the bombing could only begin a few days before *Overlord*; to do otherwise would alert the Germans to the intended assault area.

Zuckerman immediately judged the plan inadequate. It was, in his words, 'more an expression of hope' than a real plan. Interestingly, the plan did value the destruction of bridges in delaying military formations, before conceding that they were difficult targets for aircraft. The conclusion stated that attacks on rail centres offered the best prospect for successful delay of enemy reserves, but that the delay could not be expected to be more than 'several days', and in reality even fewer.

Zuckerman's knowledge of the bombing of the Italian railways was, by January 1944, well-known. At the start of January, Leigh-Mallory asked Zuckerman to produce a new plan. Using experience derived from Pantelleria and the Sicilian and Italian campaigns, Zuckerman worked quickly. At the same time, a small AEAF Bombing Committee was set up, consisting of Zuckerman, Brant, Sherrington and others, including Colonel Hughes of the EOU.

Zuckerman's plan, 'Delay and Disorganization of Enemy Movement by Rail' (often referred to as the Zuckerman Plan or Transportation Plan), emerged over January and was endorsed by Leigh-Mallory at the end of the month. The plan made the following points:

1. Although line capacity is plentiful, motive power is short… It is thus apparent that the traffic-flow potential of the system as a whole is limited by the available motive power.
2. If the enemy were deprived of the use of locomotives in a given area, and if in addition he were also deprived of the ability to use locomotives transferred from elsewhere, railway movement within the area would come to a standstill.
3. The effect upon locomotive serviceability and thus upon rail movement of eliminating facilities for day-to-day servicing (e.g. coaling, watering, clearing out fire boxes, minor running maintenance, etc.) and servicing at longer intervals (boiler washing, fire tube cleaning, and more detailed inspections) would be almost immediate.
4. At these same railway centres there is normally to be found … a considerable proportion of the total locomotives operating in the area… With some exceptions, the importance of the servicing facilities and the number of locomotives normally to

be found in the vicinity is roughly proportionate to the size and importance of the railway centres.

5. Quite apart from the importance of the servicing facilities … the railway centres themselves are essential to the handling of heavy traffic… Any interference with the elaborate telephone and signalling system, including the control of points and crossings together with the shunting and marshalling tracks or the through-lines, will affect the flow of traffic.
6. The main weight of our attacks should fall upon targets in NORTH-EAST FRANCE and BELGIUM… Among the centres listed are 4 situated on the electric traction lines from PARIS to BORDEAUX and PARIS to LE MANS, and damage could be expected to the very vulnerable electrical equipment and overhead traction cables that will be found there… By these attacks, the enemy could be faced with the necessity of diverting anything up to five to nine hundred steam locomotives.
7. The elimination of the servicing facilities would reduce the total of these available in the area by approximately two-thirds… the enemy could probably bring in a maximum of 800–1,000 locomotives into the area. Even this … would fail for lack of servicing facilities.
8. The distribution of coal … would be made extremely difficult.
9. Before the full programme of attacks had been completed, the enemy's repair organization would have been completely overwhelmed.
10. Expert opinion is that for the enemy to move the number of trains involved in lifting 3 or 4 divisions from East and PAS DE CALAIS area to west of PARIS would take at least a week, probably more.
11. Security aspect: … a series of attacks on a number of the main rail centres would not point specifically to any area.
12. There can be no question about the relative unsuitability of such other bombing targets as a specific stretch of line, or a bridge, as compared with a railway yard … certain opportunity rail targets … could probably be effectively engaged by fighter/bombers.

The plan proposed two variations:
- Target list A: an attack on 44 French and Belgian centres and 32 in western Germany.
- Target list B: an attack on 74 French and Belgian centres, with six in Germany.

The forbidding figure of Professor Frederick Lindemann, Viscount Cherwell. 'The Prof' was gifted with an ability to clarify complex scientific problems, acting as Churchill's scientific advisor during much of World War II. Cherwell was not a pleasant man and had an ability to fall out with his peers, including Solly Zuckerman. (PA Images/Alamy Stock Photo)

Regarding variant A, Zuckerman suggested that 'the sooner Western Germany is attacked, the sooner will difficulties of movement impose a considerable strain on such industry as remains to the enemy in the Rhineland… The further, therefore, the attack … is pushed Eastwards into Germany, the greater will be the effect on German war production.' This ambitious option was not chosen in early 1944, but the concept would be picked up again after D-Day.

The option selected, plan B, listed a broad swathe of railway centres running from north of the River Loire to Paris, then north-east into Belgium. These targets covered the approaches to the 'tactical area' at a range sufficient to mask the true site of the proposed landings. (The 'tactical area' for *Overlord* was approximately bounded by the River Seine to the east and the Loire to the south. To the south-east, the 'Paris–Orleans Gap' formed a funnel for rail traffic between the Seine and the Loire.) The B variant was preferable to Bomber Command, as the older Stirlings and Halifaxes were better-suited to the shorter-range operations proposed. On the other hand, it offered the Eighth Air Force little scope for making its preferred deep-penetration attacks into German airspace.

34 CAMPAIGN OBJECTIVES

Winston Churchill in the underground Map Room in which the lengthy late-night War Cabinet Defence Committee meetings ('those awful meetings', in the words of Sir Alan Brooke, Chief of the Imperial General Staff) were held in spring 1944. Although they gave an opportunity for military and scientific matters to be discussed, Churchill's domineering personality often stifled debate. (Fremantle/Alamy Stock Photo)

By including various operational factors, Zuckerman calculated that a density of four 500lb bomb strikes per acre offered the most comprehensive destruction of the railway centres. However, 500lb bombs were not economical loads for the Halifaxes and Lancasters, which could carry a large number of 1,000lb bombs without reducing the total weight of ordnance carried. The actual number of bombs dropped depended on the number of 1,000lb bombs carried, and this in turn depended on the aircraft participating.

In some cases, the estimated weight of attack would achieve the required density per acre; in others, more bombs would be needed when weather conditions, the type of marking and the size of the targets were factored into the equation. In a break with the previous principle of 'drenching' a target area, Bomber Command decided it was more economical to send the minimum number of bombers necessary against each target rather than wasting effort by sending too many aircraft. Those centres not adequately damaged, or quickly repaired, would be subjected to repeat attacks.

In summary, Zuckerman and the railway experts believed that the railway system in northern France and Belgium was operating at full stretch. Locomotives and rolling stock were old, poorly maintained and often overloaded. A series of attacks should therefore be aimed at the network's fundamental centres (the nodal points) which maintained the network's locomotives. The process was likened by Zuckerman to striking at a nervous system, until the whole became paralysed. He never claimed that the plan would stop traffic altogether, but it would impose severe dislocation, resulting in significant and ultimately fatal delays in both German reinforcements and supply. The plan called for the participation of the strategic air forces, which (together with Pointblank commitments) was expected to extend for around 60 days before D-Day.

Tedder endorsed the Zuckerman Plan from the start, and he quickly enlisted Leigh-Mallory's backing. Portal's support was more tentative at first, but he became one of the plan's supporters. Although Zuckerman suggests Portal was a supporter of the plan sometime in January, Portal told Tedder that he was still 'trying to keep an open mind' on 14 March. Eisenhower's thoughts are more mysterious, at least until well into March, when he too gave the Zuckerman Plan his backing.

The issue of command

The first problem confronting the Allied leadership was the issue of command of the air forces for *Overlord*. An early proposal from Washington, in the autumn of 1943, was to unite the strategic air forces under one commander: this would have resulted in the Supreme Allied Commander delegating authority over both USSTAF and RAF Bomber Command, probably through another American airman. Although this was not far from the structure which ultimately emerged, it was deemed unacceptable by the British Chiefs of Staff. Their counter-proposal suggested that the strategic air forces remain under the overall control of the Combined Chiefs, delegating via the Supreme Commander to Harris and Spaatz. This in its turn was rejected by the American Joint Chiefs, who maintained, correctly, that continued control of the strategic air forces by the Combined Chiefs would be slow and cumbersome.

On 16 November 1943, a directive issued by the Combined Chiefs named Leigh-Mallory as the designated Air Commander, AEAF. Leigh-Mallory seems to have assumed that he would, in Churchill's words, 'be a real commander of the air'. Yet the directive remained ambiguous, stating, 'directives as to the control of the strategic air forces will follow at a later date', adding that the AEAF should 'lend maximum support to the Strategic Air Force Offensive'. The almost simultaneous decision to group the Eighth, Ninth and Fifteenth Air Forces under the umbrella of Spaatz's USSTAF had two effects: it streamlined coordination between the three air forces and provided a strong rival hierarchy to that of the AEAF.

At the Cairo Conference in late November, Eisenhower (recently selected by Roosevelt as the designated Supreme Commander) spoke to Churchill about the need for a single, unified Mediterranean-style command. Despite his personal liking for Eisenhower, Churchill would remain obdurate almost to the end about the question of placing the control of Bomber Command under the Supreme Commander. On 5 January 1944, Eisenhower wrote to his Chief of Staff, Walter Bedell Smith, 'I suspect that the use of these air forces for the necessary preparatory phase will be particularly resisted. To support our position it is essential that a complete plan for use of all available aircraft during this phase be ready as quickly as possible.' Throughout early 1944, Eisenhower would remain adamant that his priority was to land the troops successfully in the Assault Phase and to make sure they stayed there.

Generals Eisenhower, Koenig, Bradley (US First Army) and Air Chief Marshal Tedder. Koenig, the Free French representative at Supreme Allied HQ, accepted the need for civilian casualties in 1944, as the price of liberation. Ironically, Koenig's birthplace, Caen, would be heavily damaged by Allied bombing after D-Day. (Photo by Photo12/UIG/Getty Images)

In February, Zuckerman's plan made it plain that the strategic bombers were expected to share a heavy burden of the proposed bombing programme for a lengthy period. To Spaatz, this was madness. The Pointblank offensive was poised firstly to drag the Luftwaffe into a lethal battle of attrition, guaranteeing air superiority in time for *Overlord*, and secondly to permit a simultaneous attack on the German war economy, severely or even fatally damaging it in the weeks before *Overlord*.

Although Spaatz had no personal objection to Eisenhower taking control of the USSTAF, at least for a limited period, both Spaatz and Harris were faced with the possibility of their commands being taken from them and put under Leigh-Mallory. On 1 February, Spaatz wrote, in a letter to Arnold which remained unsent, 'a decisive ending of this affair could be achieved if we have … weather conditions permitting 15 to 20 operating days in a month, four or five of them permitting visual bombing'. Spaatz went on: 'Am somewhat concerned about the shaping up of the Air command setup here… Whether or not he [Leigh-Mallory] expects to have all Strategic Air Forces under his control also, I do not know. However, the size of his headquarters indicates that possibility.' Tedder underlined this in his autobiography, writing that Spaatz would 'not accept orders, or even coordination, from Leigh-Mallory'. Moreover, Harris and Spaatz were already undertaking missions against the V-1 weapon sites in France, which were regarded as a distraction from the primary Pointblank objectives.

An incident recounted by Zuckerman possibly sheds some light on Spaatz's attitude in the spring of 1944. Zuckerman had invited Spaatz to be his guest to the High Table at Christ Church College, Oxford. After a less-than-abstemious dinner, at which he proved hugely popular, Spaatz eventually had to be helped to bed. Zuckerman claimed that Spaatz, in a moment of sudden candour, remarked:

> I'm not against the plan. I believe you are right. But what worries me is that Harris is being allowed to get off scot-free. He'll go on bombing Germany and will be given the chance of defeating her before the invasion, while I am put under Leigh-Mallory's command.

Meanwhile, Harris had already begun his own defence. On 13 January, he wrote to Portal:

> *Overlord* must now presumably be regarded as an inescapable commitment and it is therefore necessary to consider the method by which our most powerful offensive weapon, the heavy bomber force, can be brought to bear most effectively in support of it.

Harris went on to lay out his reasoning:

> Long experience of night operations has shown that it is impossible for night bombers working individually to carry out a successful and concentrated attack on even a large and clearly defined target, except under conditions of excellent visibility, bright moonlight and meagre opposition.

The pathfinders were small in number, their marking was unlikely to be sufficiently accurate and the Main Force was incapable of anything approaching precision bombing. The tempo of operations required by *Overlord* would be impossible to meet. Harris concluded:

> It is thus clear that the best and indeed the only efficient support which Bomber Command can give to *Overlord* is the intensification of attacks on suitable industrial centres in Germany as and when the opportunity offers.

In early March, Harris added that, if the bombing of cities was stopped, German industry would soon recover and the efforts over the past year would be for nothing. Zuckerman

Harris and his staff at Bomber Command HQ, High Wycombe, January–February 1944. Although Harris was resolutely opposed to attacks on French 'precision' targets, heavy losses over Germany undermined his stance. Harris eventually bowed to the inevitable and his bombers undertook the majority of the subsequent campaign. (Popperfoto via Getty Images)

asked one of his colleagues, an eminent statistician, to examine the figures used in Bomber Command's assertion. The conclusion was that if Harris continued his offensive between March and June 1944, it would at best reduce German overall output by 7 per cent. It also seemed wholly improbable that morale would be broken in that timeframe. Meanwhile, Portal was becoming less convinced by Bomber Command's claims and observed that, instead of adopting a scientific approach, Harris simply believed in 'piling the maximum on the whole structure'.

A meeting of the AEAF Bombing Committee called for 15 February was intended to clarify matters. Instead, it descended into a long, exhausting and rambling discussion, which brought Leigh-Mallory, Tedder, Spaatz, Harris and Zuckerman into open conflict.

Leigh-Mallory began by stating that he wished the strategic air forces to begin attacks as soon as possible on the *Overlord* targets in the Transportation Plan. Spaatz responded that he and Harris were still bound by the terms of the Pointblank directive, a revised version of which had only very recently come into force. Spaatz also doubted that the Luftwaffe would rise in defence of the French and western German railway centres, and as air superiority remained the primary objective of Pointblank, he felt unable to co-operate with Leigh-Mallory's suggestion. What happened next was recounted some years later by Zuckerman: 'He [Spaatz] then turned to Leigh-Mallory and asked for the date when he proposed to take control of the Strategic Air Forces in the implementation of the *Overlord* Plan. Without the slightest hesitation, Leigh-Mallory replied, "March the 1st". Spaatz's comment was: "That's all I want to know; I've nothing further to say." At least two different sets of minutes for this meeting exist. The American version, written by Colonel Hughes (and therefore not entirely impartial), dryly recorded, 'General Spaatz could not concur in a paper at cross-purposes with his present directive.'

Harris agreed with Spaatz's stance, adding that the whole paper was based on a fallacy as a similar bombing strategy on the simpler Italian system had been ineffective. Zuckerman in his reply 'expounded at considerable length', according to Hughes, pointing out that the six Italian targets attacked in no way provided a comparison with the 76 railway centres suggested by his plan. A lengthy 'discussion' ensued between Zuckerman, Harris and the

The Halifax B. III was gradually replacing the earlier marks which had been severely punished over Germany in the winter of 1943–44. As a result, the Halifax squadrons took on many of the Transportation campaign's early raids in March 1944, leaving operations over Germany to the Lancaster squadrons. (Crown Copyright, MoD)

head of Bomber Command's Operational Research Section, Dr Basil Dickens, over target marking and bombing accuracy. This tense meeting eventually broke up after making little concrete progress and with the battle lines now clearly drawn.

In truth, the encounter had really been about matters of control, rather than the best way of supporting *Overlord* itself – and the participants knew it. The deadlock appeared unbreakable. A week later, a despairing Tedder wrote to Portal, encapsulating the situation:

> I am afraid that, having started as a confirmed optimist, I am steadily losing my optimism as to how this is all going to work out… I am more and more being forced to the unfortunate conclusion that the two Strategic forces are determined not to play. Spaatz has made it abundantly clear that he will not accept orders, or even co-ordination from Leigh-Mallory, and the only sign of activity from Harris's representatives has been a series of adjustments to the records of their past bombing statistics, with the evident intention of demonstrating that they are quite unequipped and untrained to do anything except mass fire raising on very large targets… As I see it, one of the main lessons of the Mediterranean Campaign was not merely the advisability of, but the necessity for, unified Command of the Air Force. I know that is Eisenhower's view. I very much fear that if the British Chiefs of Staff and the PM are going to take up a position regarding Bomber Command which prevents that unified control, very serious issues will arise affecting Anglo-American co-operation in OVERLORD.

As the clock counted down remorselessly towards D-Day, Leigh-Mallory too became increasingly and understandably agitated over the lack of progress – particularly concerning the USSTAF. As early as 10 February, he wrote to Spaatz, listing targets in the south of France for attack, preferably by the Fifteenth Air Force. One month later, Leigh-Mallory contacted Eisenhower, expressing concern that only 28 targets had been cleared for attack. He wrote, 'we are now reaching the stage where lack of such clearance may jeopardise our chances of completing the preparatory offensive', adding that the remaining targets should be 'given unconditional clearance without delay'.

Yet there was a glimmer of hope. Eisenhower and Portal met Churchill on 29 February, and the Supreme Commander's approach began to bear fruit. Eisenhower continued to insist on a unified air command, but with his supervision of the heavy bombers passing through Tedder. Eisenhower also emphasised that Leigh-Mallory's situation 'would not be changed so far as assigned forces are concerned but those attached for definite periods of definite jobs would not come under his command'. In so doing, Eisenhower was assuring Churchill, the British Chiefs of Staff and Washington that Leigh-Mallory was effectively out of the picture and that control over Bomber Command would be devolved through Tedder.

Portal instructed Tedder to prepare the plan for the preliminary phase, when the two air forces would be pursuing Pointblank and *Overlord* objectives side-by-side. Portal would use his authority to obtain the co-operation of the strategic air forces. Churchill later wrote to the Chiefs of Staff:

> Tedder is the aviation lobe of his [Eisenhower's] brain. [Churchill clearly enjoyed an anatomical metaphor: he had previously described Tedder as 'a sort of floating kidney'.] Tedder, in his own right and as the Deputy of the Supreme Commander, is the authority responsible for making the air plan to the satisfaction of General Eisenhower.

Churchill added ominously: '[T]here can be no question of handing over the British Bomber, Fighter or Coastal Commands as a whole to the Supreme Commander and his Deputy.'

Despite his opposition, Churchill was assured that while Eisenhower must have control over Bomber Command, he had no intention of taking over Fighter or Coastal Command. On 7 March, Portal dispatched his draft for the command arrangements, which included the sentence: 'The responsibility for supervision of air operations ... should pass through the Supreme Commander.' Eisenhower mistakenly declared it to be 'exactly what we want'. The draft was passed to the Joint Chiefs in Washington, who immediately objected to the use of the word 'supervision' instead of 'command'. In a letter to Marshall, Eisenhower wrote, 'the question of exact terms and phraseology did not arise at that time but it was clearly understood that authority for operational control ... should reside in me.'

By the morning of 22 March, even Eisenhower's patience was exhausted. In his diary he stated, 'unless the matter is settled at once I will request relief from this command.' The Chiefs of Staff had in fact met that morning, and when Eisenhower heard their decision, he added a handwritten note to the diary: 'I was told the word "direction" was acceptable to both sides of the house. Amen!'

A bevy of North American P-51 Mustangs high above the overcast, Eighth Air Force, summer 1944. The Eighth's 'Little Friends' participated in the Chattanooga fighter sweeps over Germany in the two weeks before D-Day. Large claims were made for destroyed German locomotives, although later evidence showed that many were subsequently repaired. (PhotoQuest/Getty Images)

The battle for command of the air forces appeared to have been won. But even as Eisenhower was privately rejoicing, the question of the plan to be adopted in the weeks remaining before D-Day was about to take a new twist.

Choosing the right plan?

The question of whether the Transportation Plan was the correct air plan to pursue became a focal point of dispute in January. Sir Arthur Harris had, as we have seen, been against the plan from the beginning. As late as 3 April, he wrote:

> Our worst headache has been a panacea plan devised by a civilian professor whose peacetime forte is the study of the sexual aberrations of the higher apes. Starting from this sound military basis he devised a scheme to employ almost the entire British and US bomber forces for three months or more in the destruction of targets mainly in France and Belgium.

In Zuckerman's view, Harris (who enjoyed Churchill's confidence) had brought in the Air Ministry on his side (in his book, Zuckerman was unequivocal, writing that Harris's stance 'could well have wrecked *Overlord*'). Neither Harris nor Spaatz wanted a lengthy *Overlord* support campaign, whichever form it took. The publication of Zuckerman's plan simply narrowed the focus. Harris's case was weakened by the poor results accruing from the winter campaign and the heavy losses suffered by his Bomber Command. In March, under the Air Staff's instructions, Harris agreed to attack a small number of French railway centres during the moon period. These raids will be examined more closely in the next chapter. Suffice to say, their results were better than predicted by Harris and his Operational Research Section, and his argument was thus effectively undermined.

This was only the beginning. More compelling arguments against the Transportation Plan were articulated in a document produced in early March by Air Ministry Intelligence, War Office Intelligence, the Ministry of Economic Warfare and the US Enemy Objectives Unit. The main points made were:

1. It was estimated that about 64 trains per day were needed for moving reinforcements and supplies to the Normandy battle area. This figure was considered well within the capabilities of the system, even after the attacks proposed by the Transportation Plan.
2. Even if some reduction was made to the overall capacity of the network, the German authorities would cut back French economic traffic in favour of their military needs.
3. Emphasis was laid on the German readiness to make use of motor transport to compensate for rail dislocation.
4. Maintenance facilities and blocked through-lines could be quickly repaired by forced labour.
5. The Germans were 'solvent' in locomotives, due to various factors. Although some locomotives would be destroyed in the bombing, once they were dispersed (as indeed they eventually were), attrition would be insufficient to have any decisive effect.
6. Therefore, it would be 12 months before the Transportation Plan had any appreciable effect.
7. An 'interdiction' campaign was advocated, in which attacks on bridges and selected junctions would block the routes to Normandy. The memo quoted an American analysis of bombing in Italy, citing the value of cutting bridges over destroying railway centres.

In summary, the intelligence agencies argued that there was plenty of reserve in the Franco-German rail network, due to a surplus of facilities and locomotives, as well as alternative routes. Secondly, damage to important parts of the network would be repaired too quickly. It would thus be impossible for the Allied air forces to impose the effect required in the time available before *Overlord*.

The American counter-proposals

The Interdiction Plan against the French railways had already been conceived by the EOU in response to Zuckerman's plan and embodied in a paper entitled 'Outline Plan for Air Support of Overlord' on 17 February. Like Zuckerman's concept, the Interdiction Plan was based on a study of the Italian campaign, albeit with an entirely different conclusion. The crucial element was the assertion that 'the direct interdiction of communications at bridges and lines is cheaper in terms of effort and of greater duration than blocks to marshalling yards'. The resulting proposal suggested the optimum pre-D-Day attacks should be:

1. Attacks on bridges, junctions and open stretches of line, which offered suitable targets for fighter-bombers.
2. Attacks on ammunition and fuel depots, which offered suitable targets for medium and heavy bombers.

A separate, but complementary proposal which came to be known simply as the 'Oil Plan' followed. The heavy Luftwaffe losses during 'Big Week' were an immensely encouraging sign. With US heavy bombers and their escorting fighters now able to fight their way into Germany, the EOU recognised Germany's synthetic oil industry as a lucrative target. Before Big Week was over, the first EOU draft plan, 'The Use of Strategic Air Power after 1 March 1944', was completed. The core of the proposal was that the reduction of oil production would affect the entire German economy, in particular aircraft, vehicles and tanks. The paper made use of figures and estimates of the effect of such a campaign drawn from a number of intelligence sources, particularly the MEW. The EOU paper formed the basis for the USSTAF plan presented to General Spaatz on 5 March. The paper concluded that 'no other target system holds such great promise for hastening German defeat'.

The crucial point was that the two plans were complementary to one another. The Interdiction Plan called for tactical air forces, leaving the strategic air forces to concentrate on the Oil Plan. The two-fold concept provided by the EOU had an undeniable logic and elegance of design. The plan's only weakness was the indeterminate length of time needed to produce decisive results. By late March, D-Day was a little over two months away. A meeting of all the major players, scheduled for 25 March, would provide Spaatz with the opportunity he needed.

25 March: 'The great showdown'

Tedder spoke first at the meeting, advancing the merits of the Transportation Plan. He said the defeat of the Luftwaffe remained the top priority, but the remaining heavy bomber effort ought to be devoted to rail targets. Harris conceded that the continuation of area attacks could exercise only a tangential effect. Eisenhower stated that it was 'only necessary to show that there would be some reduction, however small, to justify adopting the [Transportation] plan, provided there was no alternative available'.

This was Spaatz's cue. He based his argument for the Oil Plan on three points:

1. The Transportation Plan would 'not affect the course of the initial battle and would not prevent the movement of German reserves from other fronts'.
2. Air attacks on the European rail network could not weaken the enemy's resistance in the time remaining. The Oil Plan would weaken overall resistance, hastening the success of D-Day.
3. Air attacks on railway targets would not force the Luftwaffe to fight, whereas the oil installations would be defended 'to the last fighter'.

In early 1944, Spaatz was determined to pursue his Pointblank objectives: the defeat of the Luftwaffe over Germany and the crippling of the German war economy. Despite sharp disagreements, Spaatz, Tedder and Zuckerman remained friends. (Jack Esten/Popperfoto via Getty Images)

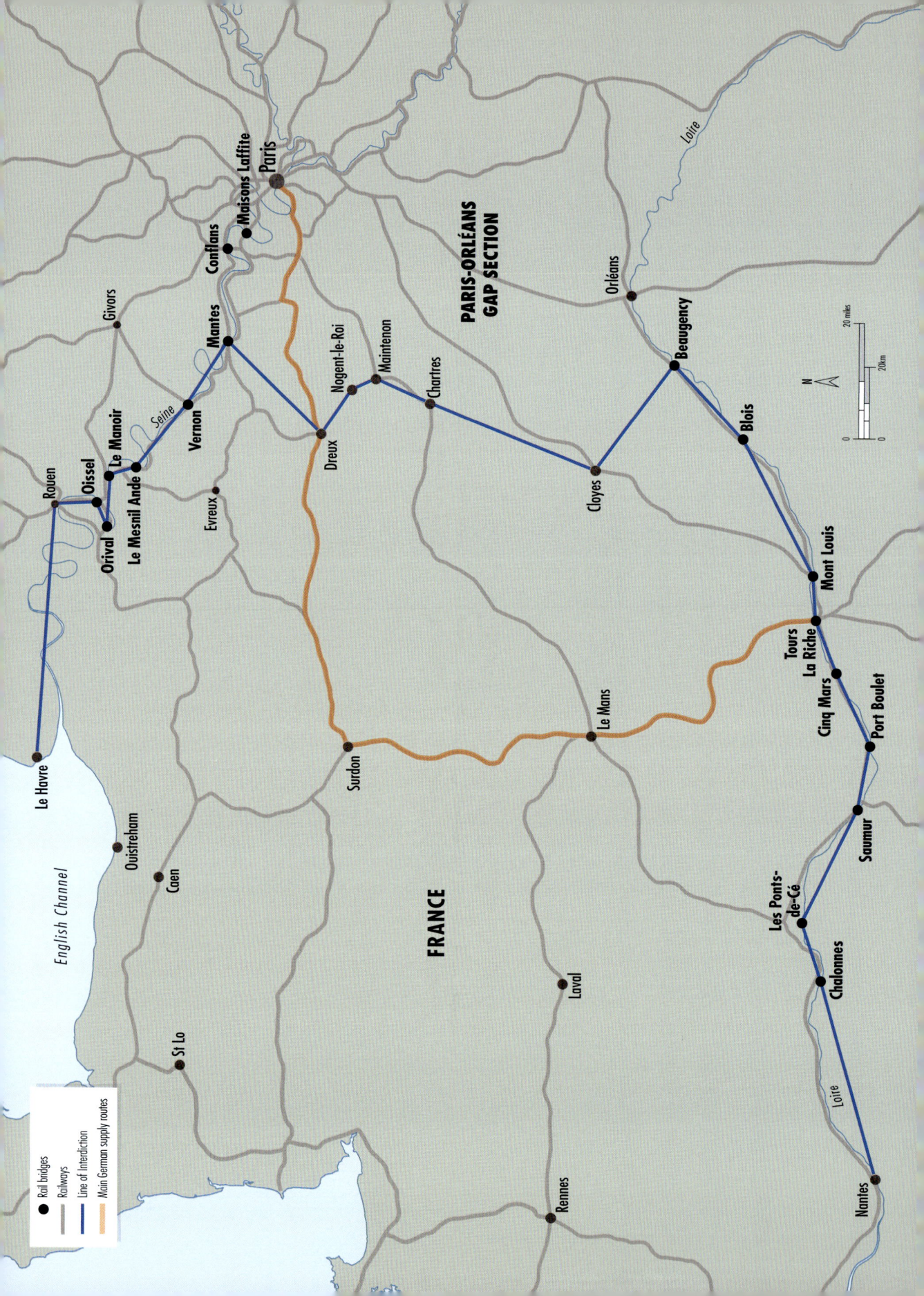

OPPOSITE THE INTERDICTION PLAN

The MEW's Oliver Lawrence was asked for an estimate for the timescale for attacks on oil installations to take effect. Lawrence replied that, if the 27 oil installations in Spaatz's plan were attacked over three months, another three months would elapse before there was a 25 per cent fall in oil production. This estimate was partially based on an assumption of large Wehrmacht oil reserves in the West.

This was the weak spot in Spaatz's argument and everyone knew it. Eisenhower wanted a plan that would assist his armies in the first 30 days after D-Day. Portal conceded that the Oil Plan should be reconsidered after the Allied armies were safely established. Meanwhile, 50 per cent of days in which visual bombing was possible were to be devoted to Luftwaffe targets. The remaining days should be used to attack transportation targets. The meeting ended with a resolution, if only tentative, that the Transportation Plan would be adopted, subject to two qualifications:

1. Spaatz would consider whether the USSTAF's allocated transportation targets could be attacked with his remaining visual effort and the effect this would have on the Luftwaffe.
2. Bombing targets in France was a delicate political matter. Therefore, the views of the Prime Minister and the Cabinet should be canvassed.

The EOU had urged Spaatz to present the Interdiction Plan within the framework of the Oil Plan. But Spaatz did not do this. In his book *Pre-Invasion Bombing Strategy: General Eisenhower's Decision of March 25, 1944*, Walt Rostow wrote: 'Eisenhower was presented with false alternatives: marshalling yards versus oil. The true alternatives were oil, plus a sustained systematic attack on bridges and dumps, versus marshalling yards.' Rostow speculated over Spaatz's (apparent) reluctance to promote the Interdiction Plan in the pivotal meeting. One possible explanation was that, like a number of Allied air commanders, Spaatz lacked confidence in *Overlord*'s chances of success. Should the landings fail, Spaatz was determined that history would show that he had done everything Eisenhower had asked of him. Colonel Hughes later wrote that 'if Eisenhower had asked him [Spaatz], in writing, to drop his bombs in the Arctic Ocean on D-Day, he would have complied'. Perhaps more convincing is the theory that Spaatz, as a friend and colleague of both Eisenhower and Tedder, would have found it uncomfortable and embarrassing to challenge the Deputy Supreme Commander's authority as a tactical airman with his own tactical air plan. Rostow also believed that Eisenhower and Tedder's decision to adopt the Zuckerman Plan stemmed from a determination to have control of the strategic air forces during the 'crisis period' of *Overlord*'s initial stages in early June. Whatever the reason, Tedder, Leigh-Mallory and Zuckerman had apparently won: Harris had bowed to the inevitable, and so had Spaatz. The EOU and other Allied agencies were left rueing the relative failure to get the air campaign they wanted.

Yet, much to Tedder and Leigh-Mallory's frustration, the USSTAF would continue to prevaricate over attacking rail centres. Pointblank remained supreme: in mid-April, it was clear that the Eighth Air Force had inflicted a crushing defeat on the Luftwaffe. On 18 and 19 April, two operations on Berlin and Kassel lost only 15 bombers from a combined total of almost 1,600 – less than

Although not universally admired by his peers, Wing Commander Leonard Cheshire's bravery and devotion to duty were unquestionable. As Commanding Officer of No. 617 Squadron, Cheshire personally led some of the earliest No. 5 Group attacks on French railway centres, including that on Juvisy on 18–19 April 1944. (Crown Copyright, MoD)

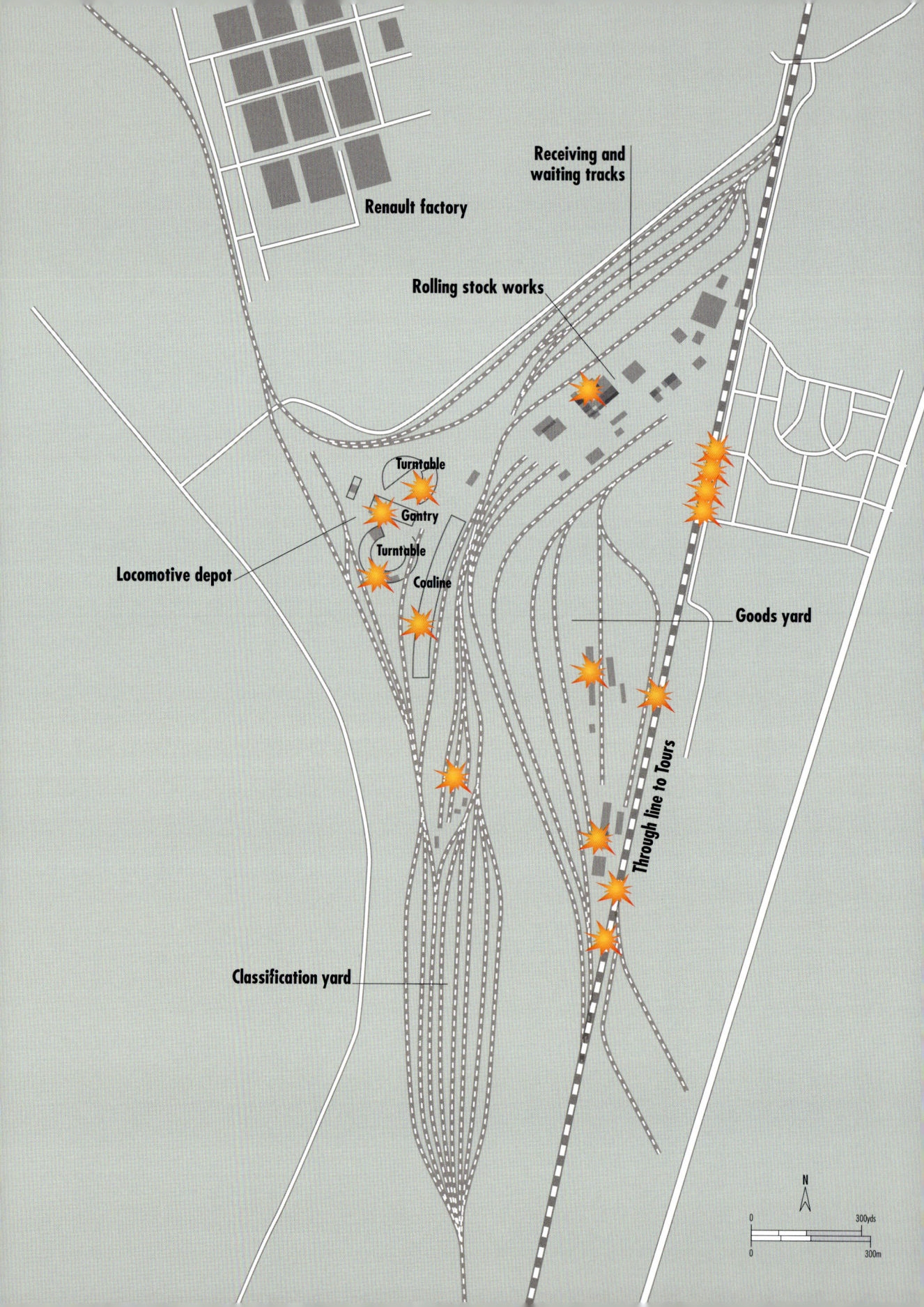

OPPOSITE A TYPICAL FRENCH RAIL CENTRE (LE MANS) WITH THE DAMAGE INFLICTED ON IT BY D-DAY

The railway centre at Le Mans was one of the most important in the *Region Ouest* and a typical example of a major French railway centre. The centre comprised large receiving and classification yards for train marshalling, a goods depot and major locomotive and rolling stock servicing facilities. Le Mans handled traffic flowing between Paris and the west coast, and between the Channel coast and the south-west of France.

Bomber Command attacked Le Mans four times before D-Day – twice in early March and twice more in late May. Although Allied intelligence summaries reported severe destruction to the locomotive facilities – the main focus of Zuckerman's plan – damage to through-lines was moderate and easily repairable. The assessment made on 6 June noted that there was 31 per cent overall damage to the buildings in the yards. The AEAF damage grading of Le Mans changed from Category C to Category A.

Later analyses noted the difference between damage sustained on the one hand and the ability to maintain at least some servicing facilities on the other. Le Mans continued to act as a major conduit for German military traffic after D-Day and the reduction in locomotive servicing capacity was partially covered by other, smaller railway centres in the region.

1 per cent. Although this was an incredible turnaround in fortunes, Spaatz knew that he needed to find targets which would force the Luftwaffe to continue fighting. This resolution revived the Oil Plan. After a tense meeting with Eisenhower, Spaatz was able to point out that the oil industry constituted part of the industry supporting the Luftwaffe. Eisenhower thus agreed to allow Spaatz to use two days of visual bombing weather over Germany to strike at synthetic oil refineries.

Morality or politics? The question of civilian casualties

However, before Eisenhower could take control of the strategic air forces and put the Transportation Plan into effect, official sanction was needed from the Prime Minister and the Cabinet. The bombing raised two connected issues. The first was the dubious morality of killing thousands of French civilians. In the words of the Foreign Secretary, Anthony Eden, 'while Russian armies defeated the enemy armies in the east, the British and Americans confined their efforts to killing French women and children'. Here, the moral question merged with the political consequences. The bombing could adversely affect Anglo-French relations for years; the more far-sighted members of the Cabinet were haunted by the possibility that post-war France could turn to a communist government. Thus, although an agreement of sorts had been reached on the plan to be adopted, its survival was jeopardised by the question: what would be the results of night and day attacks by hundreds of heavy bombers on targets which were usually located near heavily populated civilian areas?

Four days after the meeting in which Eisenhower had chosen the Transportation Plan, he wrote to Churchill, requesting clearance to be given for the listed targets. On 5 April, hours before Churchill was due to chair a Defence Committee meeting to decide whether permission should be given to Eisenhower's request, Zuckerman and Tedder were asked to respond to a Ministry of Home Security estimate which concluded that between 80,000 and 160,000 casualties could result from the bombing. Zuckerman was forthright in his dismissal of the calculations used by the paper. The figures were, in his view, nothing more than 'a deliberate effort to find an additional argument against the AEAF plan'.

The conference began at 10.30pm (the Defence Committee meetings were known by some as 'Winston's midnight follies') and, in addition to senior Cabinet ministers and the Chiefs of Staff, was attended by Tedder, Zuckerman, Lord Cherwell and Air Commodore Sidney Bufton of the Air Ministry's Directorate of Bombing Operations. The meeting got off to a rocky start when Churchill began by reading a note written for him by Cherwell, his scientific advisor, in which the Transportation Plan was referred to as 'the brain child of a biologist who happened to be passing through the Mediterranean'. At this point, an embarrassed Cherwell attempted to intervene and it was clear that until then, Churchill had

Message urgent

du Commandement Suprême des Forces Expéditionnaires Alliées
AUX HABITANTS DE CETTE VILLE

Afin que l'ennemi commun soit vaincu, les Armées de l'Air Alliées vont attaquer tous les centres de transports ainsi que toutes les voies et moyens de communications vitaux pour l'ennemi.

Des ordres à cet effet ont été donnés.

Vous qui lisez ce tract, vous vous trouvez dans ou près d'un centre essentiel à l'ennemi pour le mouvement de ses troupes et de son matériel. L'objectif vital près duquel vous vous trouvez va être attaqué incessament.

Il faut sans délai vous éloigner, avec votre famille, <u>pendant quelques jours</u>, de la zone de danger où vous vous trouvez.

<u>N'encombrez pas les routes. Dispersez-vous dans la campagne, autant que possible.</u>

PARTEZ SUR LE CHAMP !
VOUS N'AVEZ PAS UNE MINUTE A PERDRE !

Z.F.4

'LEAVE NOW! YOU DON'T HAVE A MINUTE TO LOSE!' The Allies dropped over a million air raid warning and propaganda leaflets a month over France before D-Day. This leaflet announces that major transportation centres will be attacked and urges citizens to flee the danger zone for the relative safety of the countryside. (Pictorial Press Ltd/Alamy Stock Photo)

not realised that the target of the Prof's barb was present. A research paper which used the projected estimates of casualties was then cited. According to the record, Portal rebutted the claims in detail:

> No allowance had been made for any move of the population from the target areas.
>
> It had been assumed that all bombs carried on successful missions would cause civilian casualties.
>
> When calculating the effort required, Bomber Command had multiplied the original estimate by a factor of three. Recent results [i.e. the Bomber Command attacks in early March] had shown that the plan can be achieved by one and a half times the effort first suggested.
>
> The total number of casualties included even those slightly injured. It was our experience that the sub-division of casualties was approximately 25 per cent seriously injured and 50 per cent so slightly injured as not to require hospital treatment.

A sharp exchange of views ensued. Most of those around the table, notably Eden and the Deputy Prime Minister, Clement Attlee, opposed the Transportation Plan on political grounds. Neither Cherwell nor Bufton thought the plan would prevent enough German reinforcements arriving.

The meeting decided that warnings ought to be given two hours prior to day attacks. For night raids, a warning was to be given that the population was not to sleep within two miles of likely targets. It was agreed that the bombing should continue experimentally against rail centres where there was no risk of heavy casualties. In addition, revised casualty estimates were requested and those centres where loss of life was expected to be highest were to be suspended from the list. The meeting appears to have been an unpleasant one, with Churchill tired and belligerent, especially towards Zuckerman and Tedder. Zuckerman claimed that after the meeting, Tedder remarked, 'I suppose that this might be the end, Zuck. I wonder how much it will cost to set up as a tomato grower?'

On 12 April, the revised list estimated that over 10,000 casualties were expected if the 50 most important targets were bombed. If the two major Paris rail centres at Batignolles and Le Bourget were removed from the list, the estimate would decrease to 8,840 casualties. The calculations were based on assumptions of 'no evacuation' taking place. Early operations appeared to bear out these figures. The original calculation which required four strikes per acre was revised, reducing the bomb density and therefore the expected number of casualties.

Another Defence Committee meeting was held on 13 April to review the progress of the last week. Portal presented revised figures which showed much lower casualty estimates. Moreover, reports from sources in France stated that the casualties from nine previous raids had been 1,103, compared to the estimate of 2,540 based on the new method of calculation. It therefore seemed reasonable, Portal went on, that casualties going forward would be significantly lower even than those predicted by the new estimates. Though still unhappy, Churchill conceded that casualties were less than he had feared and he sanctioned another week of attacks. A Defence Committee meeting held a week later did little but express similar sentiments, although Churchill did reveal that he was anxious for the American air forces to play their part in the campaign, otherwise the 'odium' associated with the bombing would attach solely to the RAF.

After a Cabinet meeting on 27 April, Churchill wrote to Eisenhower and deplored the heavy bomber attacks. Churchill expressed pessimism over the efficacy of the strategic bombing and pressed a new plan. This emanated from Bufton's Directorate of Bombing Operations and was in fact a mild reworking of the EOU's plan of February, advocating attacks on the Luftwaffe together with supply depots and bridges. A suspension of attacks on certain targets was imposed on 29 April, although this was lifted, at Eisenhower's insistence, on 5 May.

Although Eisenhower's reply (which was drafted by Tedder) on 2 May expressed similar arguments to those that he and Tedder had already put forward, neither Churchill nor the War Cabinet were entirely satisfied. Churchill suggested that a total limit of 10,000 French casualties should be set for the rail centre attacks. Tedder replied that although it was difficult to estimate with any reliability the current total, he thought it would be in the region of 3,000–4,000 killed.

..Croyez-vous sincèrement...

..que les Allemands n'ont plus d'avions ?..

Si la B. B. C. vous le dit en français, l'Associated Press dit en anglais (aux Anglais) : « Le raid sur Londres du 20 février par plusieurs centaines de bombardiers allemands a causé des dégâts considérables dans de nombreux districts. » Et Reuter souligne que ce bombardement est le plus violent que Londres ait subi depuis 1941.

Et ce ne sont pas encore les représailles annoncées, déclare Berlin.

A French counter-propaganda poster extolling the Luftwaffe's Operation *Steinbock*, 1944. The poster asks: 'Do you sincerely believe that the Germans have more aircraft?' As more Allied aircraft appeared over France and news of German defeats circulated, posters such as these attempted to redress the balance of public opinion. (Photo12/UIG/Getty Images)

French protests against the bombing reached London in April and May 1944, too late to affect the course of the campaign. All made broadly the same points: precision attacks on legitimate targets were welcomed, but the apparently indiscriminate high-altitude bombing associated with the USAAF was criticised. The use of delayed-action bombs was particularly disliked, it being thought that sabotage on the ground would probably be more effective in many cases than Allied bombing. Meanwhile, Vichy propaganda was capitalising on the surge in Allied unpopularity.

Three basic factors ensured the plan's survival in late April. The first was that by 26 April, 26,000 tons of bombs had already been dropped on 32 rail centres. Secondly, in their letter of 2 May, Eisenhower and Tedder made it clear that the success of *Overlord* depended on the Transportation Plan. Finally, the total of civilian casualties appeared to be significantly lower than feared.

Nevertheless, by early May, the Cabinet, motivated by the worry that it was the RAF which was bearing the responsibility for the campaign (the Eighth Air Force had barely begun its share of the attacks), agreed that the Prime Minister should send a telegram to President Roosevelt. On 7 May, he did so, writing, 'the War Cabinet share my apprehensions of the bad effect which will be produced upon the French civilian population by these slaughters… They may leave a legacy of hate behind them… The Cabinet ask me to invite you to consider the matter from the highest political standpoint.' Then, tellingly, came the final sentence:

On 6–7 March 1944, Trappes gained the unwanted honour of being the first rail centre to be attacked by Bomber Command. Damage such as this was not an objective of the Transportation Plan but an incidental, though welcome, effect. Locomotives and rolling stock were later dispersed into smaller yards and sidings. (Crown Copyright, MoD)

'Whatever is settled between us, we are quite willing to share responsibilities with you.' Roosevelt replied four days later:

> I share fully with you your distress at the loss of life… However regrettable the attendant loss of civilian lives is, I am not prepared to impose from this distance any restriction on military action by the responsible commanders that in their opinion might militate against the success of "Overlord" or cause additional loss of life to our Allied forces of invasion.

The President's response, Churchill conceded, 'was decisive'.

THE CAMPAIGN

On 15 April, the duties of the Allied air forces were enumerated in the Allied Expeditionary Air Force's 'Overall Air Plan':
1. To maintain air superiority over the battle area.
2. To provide reconnaissance.
3. To disrupt enemy communications and channels of supply.
4. To support the landing and subsequent advance.
5. To attack enemy naval forces.
6. To provide airlift for airborne forces.

These tasks were to be delivered in four phases:
1. The Preliminary Phase. The attainment of air superiority, the reduction of German war potential and the weakening of morale. This first phase had been partially met by Pointblank.
2. The Preparatory Phase. In this there were two broad and overlapping categories:
    - The strategic operations included the completion of Pointblank and the strategic portion of the Transportation Plan. This was scheduled to begin about three months before D-Day.
    - The tactical operations, among many other duties, included the intensification of attacks on key points of the rail network in closer proximity to the assault area. This was scheduled to begin some three weeks before D-Day. Operation *Fortitude* (the *Overlord* deception plan) required that for every target attacked in the Normandy area, two more had to be attacked elsewhere.
3. The Assault Phase covered operations on D-Day itself.
4. The Subsequent to the Assault Phase covered operations after D-Day. The exact nature of these remained unknown before D-Day.

Ninth Air Force Douglas A-20 Havocs, June 1944, after bombing a supply depot. Attacks on such targets were always part of the overall air plan for *Overlord*. They may have exacerbated the German logistical difficulties which already existed, particularly in shortages of petrol, oil/lubricants and ammunition. (Galerie Bilderwelt/Getty Images)

On 17 April, Eisenhower's directive to the strategic air forces was issued:

Directive by the Supreme Commander to USSTAF and Bomber Command for Support of OVERLORD during the Preparatory Period
  Overall mission
  The overall mission of the strategical Air Forces remains the progressive destruction and dislocation of the German military, industrial and economic system, and the destruction of vital elements of lines of communication. In the execution of this overall mission the immediate objective is first the destruction of German air combat strength, by the successful prosecution of the Combined Bomber offensive. Our re-entry on the Continent constitutes the supreme operation for 1944; all possible support must, therefore, be afforded to the Allied Armies by our Air Forces to assist them in establishing themselves in the lodgement area...
  The particular mission of the strategical air forces prior to the OVERLORD assault is:
  To deplete the German air force and particularly the German fighter forces, and to destroy and disorganise the facilities supporting them.
  To destroy and disrupt the enemy's rail communications, particularly those affecting the enemy's movement towards the OVERLORD lodgement area.

This somewhat vague document could, and would, be interpreted differently in the forthcoming campaign. For Bomber Command, the extent to which it actually participated in the preparatory phase was left to the goodwill of its Commander-in-Chief. To the surprise of some, Harris would in fact devote himself wholeheartedly to the *Overlord* plan. For the USSTAF it was different, and Spaatz would continue to attack aviation and oil targets across Germany.

Allocation of targets by the AEAF

As the campaign went on, AEAF HQ used photo-reconnaissance imagery to evolve a categorisation of target assessments:
- Category A: Sufficiently damaged to require no more attention until further notice.
- Category A+: Eliminated so far as heavy bombers were concerned but possibly requiring daylight attack by medium bombers to complete the destruction of particular facilities.
- Category B: Severely damaged but retaining vital installations and requiring repeat attack on lower priority than Categories C and D.
- Category C: Attacked but with little or no material damage and requiring repeat attack on highest priority.
- Category D: Rail centres authorised for attack but so far not bombed and to be placed at second priority.
- Category E: Rail centres in plan but not yet cleared for attack.

The main attacks by heavy and medium bombers were made against the following centres, together with attacks against smaller junctions within their boundaries:
- The Nantes–Angers–Saumur–Tours–Orléans area, to cut rail traffic from southern France.
- The Orléans–Châteaudun–Chartres–Étampes–Dreux area, to cut traffic from south-eastern and eastern France.
- The Paris junctions, to cut traffic from north-eastern and eastern France.
- The Rennes–Pontaubault area, to cut traffic from west of Brest and the Brest peninsula.

Bomber Command was allocated rail centres in Belgium, north-west France and Paris.

Targets listed by order of priority in SHAEF directive, 21 April 1944			
Targets allocated to Bomber Command			
Block	Target	Priority within Block/ status after previous attack	Target suspended, 29 April–5 May
Block C (first priority) The main Paris centres	Paris–Batignolles	1	X
	Paris–La Plaine	1	X
	Paris–Le Bourget	2	X
	Villeneuve St Georges	3	X
	Paris–Noisy-le-Sec	4 (Category B)	X
	Paris–Juvisy	Category A	X
	Vaires	Category A	
	Trappes	Category A	
Block B (second priority) Belgian and north-eastern French routes	Tergnier	1	X
	Lens	2	X
	Courtrai	3	X
	Lille–Fives	4	X
	Lille–La Deliverance	Category A	X
Block A (third priority) A line running north–south on the Belgian-German border	Aulnoye	1	
	Ghent	2	X
	Ottignies	3	
	Laon	4 (Category B)	X
Block D (fourth priority)	Montzen	1	
	Miramas	2	
	Rouen–Sotteville	3 (Category B)	X
	Boulogne-sur-Mer	4	X
	Tours–St Pierre des Corps	Category A	X
	Amiens–Longeau	Category A	X
	Le Mans	Category A	X

In deference to Spaatz's wishes, the Eighth Air Force was to make deeper penetrations into enemy air space in an effort to bring the Jagdwaffe (Fighter Force) to battle, and was accorded targets in Belgium and eastern France. Further rail targets in Germany were listed separately. The Italian-based B-17s and B-24s of the Fifteenth Air Force played little part in the campaign save for attacks on 25, 26 and 27 May on rail centres in the south of France.

Targets allocated to the Eighth Air Force			
Block	Target	Priority within Block	Target suspended, 29 April–5 May
Block D (first priority)	Metz	1	
	Thionville	2	
	Strasbourg–Hausbergen	3	
	Sarreguemines	4	
	Luxembourg	5	
	Blainville	6	

table continued overleaf

Block B (second priority)	Mulhouse (main station)	1	
	Mulhouse (Nord)	2	
	Épinal	3	X
	Mulhouse (Ile Napoleon)	4	
	Belfort	4	
Block A (equal third priority with Block C)	Brussels–Sharbeck	1	
	Brussels–Midi	2	
	Liège–Guillemines	3	X
	Liège–Kinkempois	3	
	Liège–Renory	3	
Block C (equal third priority with Block A)	Troyes	1	
	Châlons-sur-Marne	2	
	Reims	3	
	Nancy	3	
	Chaumont	4	

The medium bombers of the two tactical air forces were assigned smaller rail centres in northern and western France.

Targets allocated to Ninth Air Force			
Block	Target	Priority within Block	Target suspended, 29 April–5 May
Block A (equal first priority with Block E)	Mohon (Shed)	1	
	Hirson	2	
	Mohon (Mézières)	3	
	Somain	3	
	Béthune	3	
	Arras	3	
	Douai	4	
	Cambrai	5	
Block E (equal first priority with Block A)	Mantes–Gassicourt	1	
	Creil	2 (Category B)	X
Block B (equal second priority with Block D)	St Ghislain	1	
	Haine St Pierre	1	
	Charleroi–Monceau	2	
	Charleroi–Montignies	2	
	Charleroi–St Martin	2	
	Namur–Ronet	3 (Category B)	
Block D (equal second priority with Block B)	Louvain	1	
	Malines	2	
	Hasselt	3 (Category B)	
Block C (third priority)	Valenciennes	1	
	Tournai	2	X
	Mons	3	X
	Tourcoing	4	
Block F (fourth priority)	Aarschot	All of equal priority well below priority of all other targets	
	Antwerp/Dam		X
	Busigny		
	Calais		

Bomber Command's operations before the 25 March meeting

Following the ill-tempered meeting of 25 February, Harris agreed to take on the 12 French and Belgian rail targets requested for clearance by Leigh-Mallory during the March moon period, provided he received the necessary authority from the Air Ministry. A few days later, the Air Staff decided to test Harris's assertion and sent a directive containing the names of various small targets in France, including six railway targets cleared for attack using Oboe ground marking in moonlight periods. Harris lost no time and, on the night of 6–7 March, dispatched 260 Halifaxes against Trappes, south-west of Paris. Four more operations followed during the March moon period: two raids on Le Mans and another two against Amiens. The five attacks, plus a sixth, smaller effort against Laon, were judged successful, with serious damage being caused in the yards and enormous numbers of locomotives and stock being destroyed. French casualties were thought to be low: 79 civilians were estimated to have been killed in the two attacks on Le Mans. Bomber Command lost only six aircraft in the six attacks.

Bomber Command then made a further three small attacks during the remainder of the month: Aulnoye, Courtrai and Vaires. The marking of Aulnoye and Courtrai was inaccurate and neither centre was badly damaged. Much of the bombing on Courtrai fell in the town and killed an estimated 252 people. The attack on Vaires was made in bright moonlight by 84 Halifaxes. Two ammunition trains exploded, devastating much of the surrounding area, including a troop train parked alongside, and killed an estimated 1,270 German troops.

Bomber Command's initial operations from the night of 9–10 April mainly concentrated on the western and Parisian rail centres. After 10–11 April, poor weather conditions meant Bomber Command did not venture over the French yards in strength – or anywhere else – for almost a week. Very frequent attacks were then launched until early May (between 18–19 April and 12–13 May, the bombers carried out 35 operations on 15 nights). The suspension of attacks against 18 targets, enforced on 29 April, was lifted on 5 May. After another period of rain and fog over the UK, the campaign resumed on 19–20 May. From this point until D-Day, the bombing was extended against the lines running to Paris from the east and the 'avoiding' routes south of Paris. This included three attacks against Aachen at the end of May – the only rail target in Germany struck by Bomber Command in the pre-*Overlord* campaign. Overall, the bomber effort rose from 25 attacks in April to 32 in May.

Opening night

On the night of 6–7 March 1944, Bomber Command delivered the first attack of the Transportation campaign when 267 Halifaxes from Nos. 4 and 6 Groups bombed the railway centre at Trappes, south-west of Paris. The operation was planned in two phases: the first wave would attack the western part of the yards from 8.45pm; the second attack, on the eastern end, was scheduled to begin at 9.11pm. Four de Havilland Mosquitoes of 8 (Pathfinder) Group conducted blind Oboe marking (codenamed *Musical Paramatta*) on both aiming points. The night was clear, bathing Trappes in moonlight.

This illustration shows the moment the second attack was opened, slightly late, at 9.13pm by Mosquito B. XVI, serial ML957, of 109 Squadron, flown by Flying Officer A. A. Dray and Flight Lieutenant W. G. Finlay. The last Halifaxes from the first wave were completing their bomb runs as Dray and Finlay released a pair of red Target Indicators from 26,000ft over the eastern aiming point.

Returning crews described the bombing as well concentrated. The record book for 105 Squadron stated, 'all the marking aircraft were successful, and the heavies … reported the TIs [Target Indicators] as being well concentrated and very accurate. The yards were clearly seen in the bright moonlight and the absence of cloud made the TIs plainly visible. The bombing, especially in the second phase, was extremely accurate and most of the bombs were seen to fall right across the markers.'

Trappes was out of action for three days, after which limited service was restored to one of the main through-lines. Twenty locomotives were destroyed and 69 more damaged. The attackers suffered no losses.

OPPOSITE THE NO.5 GROUP TARGET-MARKING METHOD

Revised tactics

The disaster suffered by Bomber Command on the Nuremberg operation on 30–31 March, with the loss of almost 100 aircraft, caused a revision to Bomber Command tactics. The practice of dispatching one large bomber stream against a single target was abandoned, and from 1 April, Harris instructed that multiple targets were to be attacked with the object of dividing and confusing the enemy night-fighter defences, together with complicated and varying routeing of the different bomber streams. No. 8 Group did not have the aircraft to support the policy of multiple targeting and Harris therefore decreed that the individual Groups would be responsible for their own marking methods. To Donald Bennett's displeasure, three of his squadrons, 83 and 97 Lancaster Squadrons and 627 Mosquito Squadron for low-level marking duties, were detached to operate with Cochrane's No. 5 Group. Although this was a case of No. 5 Group receiving preferential treatment, it was not without reason. The Group was large enough to attack two targets in one night, and had the experience and expertise necessary for marking its own targets.

Bombing accuracy

Paradoxically, the Transportation Plan required the most accurate bombing possible, yet relied overwhelmingly on Bomber Command, the least precise of the Allied air forces. The more accurate the bombing, the fewer the aircraft needed per attack. This in turn meant that more targets could be struck in a night of operations, giving a better economy of effort. The overall bombing 'average radial error' predicted before the campaign by the Bomber Command Operational Research Section was 640yds (a prediction that 50 per cent of bombs aimed would fall within a radius of 640yds around the aiming point). In reality, the error was slightly worse, at 680yds. The assumption that 70 per cent of bombs would be correctly aimed was reduced in reality to just 55 per cent. Although these figures were considered a good return for Bomber Command, especially by the standard set by the area bombing

Aulnoye after the attacks of 10–11 and 27–28 April. The servicing facilities are badly damaged, the yards are pock-marked by hundreds of craters and rolling stock has been wrecked. The AEAF classed Aulnoye's damage at 'Category A' by D-Day. Compare this image to that on page 8. (Crown Copyright, MoD)

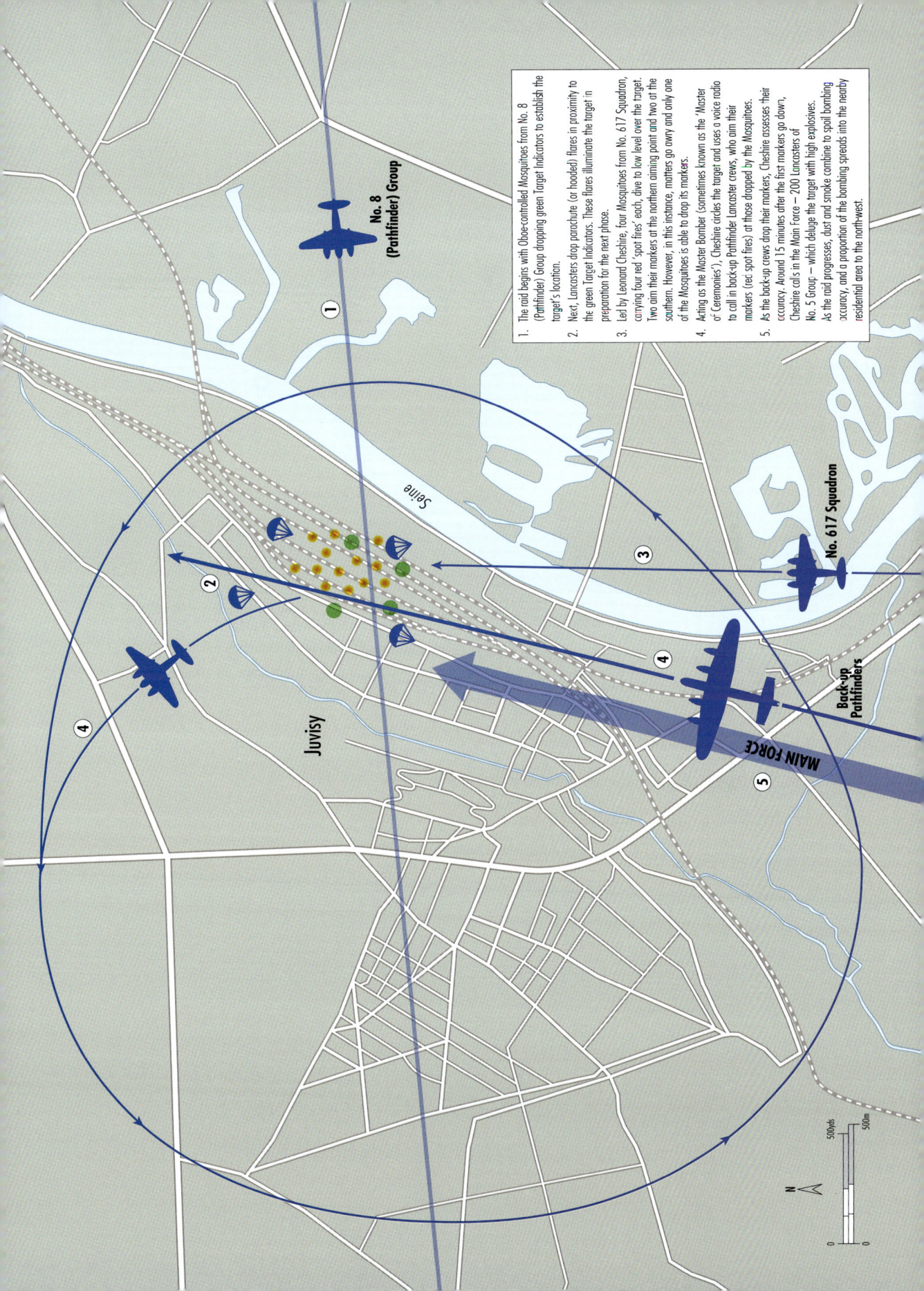

This image of Juvisy on 18–19 April illustrates the problem presented to the attackers. Smoke and dust drift from the yards (seen on the far side of the Seine) amid the glare from a profusion of Target Indicators and photo flash bombs. The bombing eventually spread into the residential housing adjoining the yards. (Associated Press/Alamy Stock Photo)

campaign, they represented bad news for those living near the rail centres. A number of the centres selected for attack, especially those in the industrial north of France, were subject to haze created by this industry, which obscured target marking. In addition, it was obvious from early in the campaign that reattacking centres was going to be necessary, either because the initial estimate of the bombs necessary to destroy a centre was too low or because the centre was repaired and service resumed.

The early operations had used the Oboe ground marking method. Since the majority of rail targets were elongated or complex in shape, two aiming points were normally selected, and these were then marked individually and successively bombed in separate waves. However, Harris by this stage permitted the individual Groups to practice their own techniques, and the No. 5 Group attack on Tours on the night of 10–11 April employed the visual ground marking technique used in previous attacks on small industrial targets.

The various marking techniques used for the remaining 18 attacks in April met with mixed success. The No. 5 Group method was employed again in the Group's attacks on the major Parisian rail centres of Juvisy (the main depot for the electrified line southwards to Bordeaux and Limoges) on 18–19 April and La Chapelle on 20–21 April. The attacking force detailed for La Chapelle was split into two waves, which bombed separate aiming points one hour apart. Evaluation showed that while the No. 5 Group method depended on highly trained and experienced crews, it did on average offer the most accurate results.

Another technique, 'Controlled Oboe', was first tried on 10–11 April in the attack on Aulnoye, being repeated on several operations towards the end of April. The target was marked by Oboe-guided Mosquitoes dropping green Target Indicators before zero hour. Parachute flares then illuminated the area and, in the light of these, the 'master of ceremonies' dropped red Target Indicators visually, then directed the back-up crews and the Main Force to bomb the best-placed markers. Although not as accurate as the No. 5 Group method, Controlled Oboe marking could be employed in conditions of poor visibility.

A third option was 'Musical Newhaven', which was similar to the No. 5 Group technique but used Target Indicators instead of spot fires. Unsurprisingly, while an improvement over conventional Oboe ground marking, it was less impressive than either the No. 5 Group or Controlled Oboe methods. The improvement in accuracy taken as a whole was considerable: between March and May, bomb densities around the aiming points improved by 165 per cent.

The campaign intensifies

On 18–19 April, 181 Lancasters and Halifaxes made a complex hybrid Newhaven/Oboe ground marking attack on the important junction at Noisy-le-Sec, north of Paris. The Bomber Command report noted that 'there was some undershooting on the line of approach', which caused 'some damage' to the south of the town. The attack was so devastating that the yard was not completely restored until 1951. The undershooting, on the other hand, killed 464 people and injured another 370. A similar attack on Tergnier on the same night went badly awry. One Mosquito marked 1,500yds to the north-west of the yards, the other 700yds to the south-west. Unfortunately, the Master Bomber ordered the Main Force to bomb the south-western Indicators. Only a few bombs hit the target, the rest falling over the town.

A raid by 112 Halifaxes on Somain on the night of 30 April–1 May was compromised when the pathfinder Mosquitoes arrived late. To worsen matters, the first Target Indicators fell a mile away from the aiming point, over the western boundary between the yard and the town. The Main Force, waiting for the first Target Indicators, had bombed by the time the Master Bomber had managed to correct the problem.

Although the marking in an attack on Malines in Belgium on 1–2 May was 'accurate and well-concentrated', a ground haze quickly obscured the target and even the Bomber Command report admitted that the bombing became scattered. The results were particularly tragic, with 171 civilians killed and another 123 injured.

A similarly heavy haze over the Belgian junction at Hasselt on 11–12 May forced the Master Bomber to stop the attack after 39 aircraft had already bombed. Although conditions were much clearer over Boulogne on the same night, the bombing by No. 6 Group became very scattered. A follow-up next night on Hasselt was not much more successful. A raid on 19–20 May against Amiens found the target covered by 10/10ths cloud and the attack was halted by the Master Bomber after just 37 Lancasters had completed their runs.

A Controlled Oboe ground marking operation on 28–29 May against the Loire town of Angers by Lancasters of No. 3 Group was initially praised in the Bomber Command report – 'the Master Bomber marked the target accurately, and crews achieved a good concentration' – but the reality was badly scattered bombing which killed 254 people and injured another 220.

In general, the bombing improved as the campaign developed. The No. 5 Group attack on La Chapelle already mentioned hit a barracks at Clignancourt to the south-east of the yard, killing an unknown number of German troops. A Controlled Oboe ground marking attack against Achères by 106 Halifaxes on 30 April–1 May benefited from accurately placed markers and clear instructions from the Master Bomber. On the following night, St Ghislain and the Chambly rail depot were bombed in similar Controlled Oboe attacks. The Master Bomber arrived late over St Ghislain, but his deputy took over and directed the early stages of the attack. Over Chambly, the initial Oboe marking was poor but the Master Bomber was able to retrieve the situation by ordering the Main Force to aim at his own markers.

An oblique photo-reconnaissance image offers a closer look at the Juvisy rail centre after 18–19 April. The vulnerable electric catenary wires are down and some of the wrecked rolling stock appears to have been cleared from the lines. In the foreground, workmen can be seen pausing as the aircraft passes overhead. (Crown Copyright, MoD)

Bomber Command's first large-scale operation, 10–11 April 1944

On the night of 10–11 April 1944, Air Chief Marshal Sir Arthur Harris unleashed Bomber Command against five railway centres in France and Belgium. The attacks, although employing various target-marking methods, enjoyed only mixed success, and the night brought Bomber Command's first major losses of the campaign.

Key:

- Allied inbound
- Allied outbound
- Axis fighters

 Axis airfields

 Allied downed bombers

EVENTS

1. 1045hrs. 124 Halifaxes of No. 6 Group attack the railway centre at Ghent. An earlier raid by 36 Mosquitoes on Hannover has diverted night fighters. One Halifax is lost crossing the coast.

2. 1150hrs. The Mosquitoes from Ghent arrive over Tergnier to open an attack for 157 Halifaxes of No.4 Group. Despite problems with the Oboe equipment, the marking of both points is good and the yards are badly damaged.

3. Midnight. Night fighters of III/NJG 1, III/NJG 4 and I/NJG 6, from Juvincourt and Laon-Athies, are fed into the bomber stream as it departs for the coast. Hptm Kurt Fladrich of NJG 4 shoots down the first Halifax, followed by a second 25 minutes later. Eight more Halifaxes are lost, half to Uffz Leopold Weinberger, who destroys four in less than 15 minutes.

4. 0130hrs. As the Halifaxes stream back to their Yorkshire bases, 180 Lancasters from No. 5 Group cross into France in two waves, bound for the railway centre at Tours. The bombers, using the No. 5 Group method, make an accurate attack on the first aiming point. The second wave finds the target largely obscured by smoke. Very heavy damage is caused to the centre of Tours. Just one Lancaster is hit by flak and crashes over the target.

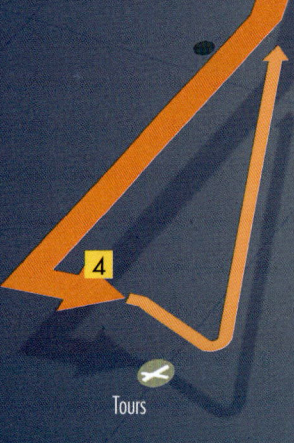
Tours

EVENTS

5. 0217hrs. A two-wave attack against Aulnoye by 129 Lancasters of No. 1 Group begins. Oboe Mosquitoes mark the target in green and Master Bombers follow with red markers, however the marking is poor and one of the Master Bombers drops an indicator quarter of a mile from the aiming point and then orders an attack on the green markers.

6. 0220hrs. Hptm Helmut Bergmann of NJG 4 is guided into the bomber stream as it returns over north-west France. His first victim goes down at 0220hrs. Over the next 45 minutes, Bergmann shoots down another six Lancasters.

7. 0234hrs. The Oboe-marking for the second part of the Aulnoye attack is late and, before it begins, the previous Master Bombers drop red indicators intended for the northern aiming point, nearer to the southern point. The Oboe Mosquitoes then drop green markers and the Main Force is ordered to bomb the latter marking. In the confusion, many bombs fall in open country to the north and south of the target.

8. 0335hrs. The final attack of the night is directed against Laon. Despite close proximity to Laon-Athies airfield, negligible opposition is encountered. The marking by the Oboe Mosquitoes is inaccurate. Much of the bombing goes down over the western edge of the yards, where fortunately it causes few casualties.

Smoke and dust obscure the railway centre near the Belgian town of Hasselt, under attack from B-26 Marauders of the Ninth Air Force, April 1944. Clear visibility made precision attacks possible, but such conditions were rare over North-West Europe. (Fox Photos/Hulton Archive/Getty Images)

When the Halifaxes of No. 6 Group arrived over Louvain on 12–13 May, it was covered by a thick haze similar to that which had afflicted the attack on Hasselt the night before. Fortunately, on this occasion the marking was clearly visible and 'the attack fell squarely on the target'. Near the beginning of the attack, a massive explosion was seen, sufficient to obscure the target markers, with the result that 15 aircraft returned without dropping their bombs.

Controlled Oboe ground marking was used over Orléans on 19–20 May. Despite some undershooting early in the raid, the Master Bomber was able to correct the bombing. A 'huge orange explosion', which obscured the target with smoke, forced the raid to be suspended in its closing stages. On the same night, Le Mans (a major marshalling yard and junction, serving traffic running between Paris and Brittany and linking Bordeaux and the south of France to Normandy) was attacked by Lancasters of No. 3 Group. The Master Bomber ordered the attack to go in under a 8–10/10ths cloud base over the target, and although the early bombing was reportedly well concentrated, the attack deteriorated in the later stages. This may have been due to the loss of both the Master Bomber and his deputy in a collision over the target.

The No. 5 Group technique was used against the Nantes junction on 27–28 May. The junction lay within a heavily built-up area on the River Loire. Fortunately, 'the early bombing was so accurate', noted the Bomber Command report, 'that the A/P [Aiming Point] was quite invisible after a few minutes, and later arrivals were ordered to bring their bombs back'. The attack 'fell squarely on the target, no less than 80 hits being scored on the flyovers and junctions, and 26 more on the railway sidings'.

Between 6–7 March and D-Day, Bomber Command launched 68 operations and dropped 44,356 tons of bombs against 39 separate transportation targets, 38 per cent of its total effort for the period.

Bomber Command losses, 1 March–31 May 1944						
Month	Total sorties	Total losses	Total loss rate	Transportation Plan sorties	Transportation Plan losses	Transportation Plan loss rate
March	9,031	283	3.1%	1,591	7	0.44%
April	9,873	214	2.2%	3,810	66	1.7%
May	11,353	274	2.4%	4,016	108	2.7%
1–5 June	1,612	27	1.7%	186	16	12.5%
Totals	31,869	798	2.4% (average)	9,603	197	1.9% (average)

The night fighters react

The campaign over Germany continued in earnest until the Nuremberg disaster at the end of March. Even then, Bomber Command continued to make sporadic attacks on German towns until 23 May. By the end of March, the majority of the Luftwaffe's night-fighter units had been relocated in the south-west of Germany to enable interception of bomber streams on their inbound and outbound routes for cities such as Frankfurt, Nuremberg, Stuttgart and Munich.

Although Bomber Command's overall loss rate decreased by about a third between March and April, the loss rate over France almost quadrupled. The overall loss rate increased slightly in May but jumped to 2.7 per cent over France – which was not far below the rate for the disastrous month of March. Most of the losses were due to night-fighter action. Flak accounted for roughly between a quarter and a fifth of all losses over the period.

The St Pierre des Corps rail centre at Tours was badly damaged by 180 Lancasters, bombing in two waves, on 10–11 April. While the first force bombed accurately, the second found the target obscured by smoke, causing bombs to be scattered in the area around the target. (Crown Copyright, MoD)

Several factors were responsible for the increase in Bomber Command's loss rate. One was the swift reorientation of the Luftwaffe's night-fighter units in April, when it became clear that France had become the main focus of attention. Night-fighter assembly beacons were extended into France and Belgium. This was coupled with the issuing of increased numbers of the more effective Lichtenstein SN-2 radars into the Luftwaffe's night fighters. Finally, and by Harris's own admission, evasion and decoy tactics were nearing their limit. It was scarcely any longer possible to fool the German night-fighter controllers with sudden route doglegs, simultaneous attacks, feints or spoof raids. Despite the losses inflicted on Bomber Command, the Nachtjagd was unable to affect the course of the campaign in any way. The high tide had been reached in March 1944 and Bomber Command would not suffer such losses again.

The Eighth Air Force throws its hat into the ring

It can be said that the first attack of the Transportation Plan by the Eighth Air Force was the mission against the giant railway centre at Hamm in north-west Germany on 22 April. The attack proved costly to the Eighth. It was late in the day when the Liberators of the Second Division returned to their bases. A number of Messerschmitt Me 210 twin-engine fighters followed the B-24s back to East Anglia, and in the darkness destroyed 14 Liberators as they landed. The Hamm mission was followed by an abortive strike on Mannheim on 25 April, and then the yards at Blainville and Châlons on 27 April. Both the USAAF and Luftwaffe had lost heavily. The Eighth Air Force's losses were 25 per cent over April, but, in the same month, the Luftwaffe lost 489 fighter pilots and trained only another 396. The situation could only go one way.

Over the next four weeks, the Eighth mounted more than 70 attacks on railway targets in Belgium, eastern France and western Germany. The campaign was interspersed with missions which flew deep into German airspace in an effort to bring the Luftwaffe to battle. The first oil industry targets were attacked on 12 May, with further missions against refineries on 28 and 29 May. These missions were strongly opposed by the Luftwaffe, and the attacks began a process which would dramatically diminish German oil production. Spaatz had maintained from the start that he did not believe the Luftwaffe would fight to defend the French railways in daylight. The ensuing campaign proved him correct.

An inaccurate raid on Hasselt on 11–12 May, halted prematurely, was the 100th sortie of Lancaster R5868, 'S-Sugar', of 467 Squadron, seen being celebrated in this photograph. The night also saw the death of the squadron commander and his crew on their 30th and final operation. Today, 'S-Sugar' resides at the RAF Museum, Hendon. (Imperial War Museums, TR 1795)

The true start date for the Eighth's Transportation campaign was 1 May, when railway centres in Belgium and north-east France were bombed. The bombers were well protected and the Luftwaffe prudently avoided combat. A week later, B-24s made an unsuccessful attack on Liège. Cloud covered much of the yards, and those B-24s which did bomb missed their target. An attempt by fighters to engage them was unsuccessful, some of the Jagdgruppen only succeeding in becoming entangled with a sweep by 2nd TAF Spitfires.

A massive effort on 11 May against 13 rail targets across Belgium, eastern France and western Germany was again marred by indifferent bombing results. Fighter units from Luftflotte Reich were scrambled, but most were ordered to land when the bombers' targets became obvious. Some combats did take place and the Kommodore of JG 1, Obst Walter Oesau, became a famous casualty when he was killed by P-38 Lightnings. The day ended with the Americans writing off 20 bombers and fighters, while the Luftwaffe lost nine pilots killed and 25 fighters.

The Eighth made its biggest effort so far on 23 May, when over 1,000 bombers were dispatched to make visual bombing attacks against rail targets in Germany and France. The Luftwaffe fighter controllers were tricked into believing that Berlin or Leipzig were the targets, and an attempted interception of bombers by III/JG 26 near Colmar was broken off in the face of the Mustang escort. Four days later, Doolittle's bombers again targeted western Germany, in conjunction with extensive fighter sweeps over France and Belgium. Although Luftflotte Reich enjoyed some success, Luftflotte 3 had little choice but to vector its fighters inland to keep them out of the way. More missions on 31 May had little effect. Cloud caused some missions to be aborted and marred the bombing of the rest. Moreover, the Luftwaffe largely refused to meet the large American formations. On 2 June, despite extensive cloud cover, attacks were launched against the Parisian yards on the Grande Ceinture.

Overall effort for the campaign

The Eighth's participation in the campaign during May 1944 was as much about continuing the pressure on the Luftwaffe as it was about *Overlord*. Overall, the campaign had been something of a disappointment: attacks on French targets had not brought the Luftwaffe

The remains of a No. 6 Group Halifax B. III tail section in the marshalling yard at Noisy-le-Sec, 19 April 1944. This was one of 11 losses sustained that night by Bomber Command. The French raids are sometimes portrayed as 'milk runs', but the Luftwaffe night fighters, although in decline, remained a formidable presence. (Keystone-France/Gamma-Rapho via Getty Images)

to battle, and the bombing itself was mixed in its results. Between 17 April and 5 June, the Eighth Air Force dropped 15,699 tons of bombs on rail targets, 22 per cent of its total tonnage for the period. This contrasts with the 24,125 tons of bombs (34 per cent of its effort) against aircraft factories and airfields. The Eighth Air Force lost 420 aircraft in April and another 376 in May, while Luftflotte Reich lost 546 fighter pilots in April and May. If the Eighth had launched further incursions into Germany instead of attacking targets over France, then the Luftwaffe's fighter losses would have been even greater.

The campaign continues

Although Leigh-Mallory claimed the Transportation Plan to be complete by early June, the story did not end there. Not only the tactical air forces but also the strategic forces were required to maintain the pressure on the transportation system after the Allies had landed. The main difference between the pre- and post-D-Day campaigns was that the air forces no longer bombed to a pre-planned programme of targets. Instead, targets were selected by SHAEF for bombing the following day. Zuckerman's original concept increasingly blurred into a tactical campaign, albeit one performed by strategic bombers. The lion's share of the continued bombing of the rail centres was undertaken by Bomber Command, which dropped 66 per cent of the total tonnage. Zuckerman wrote a generous tribute to Bomber Command and its leader in his diary on 9 July:

> The amazing thing is that Harris, who was even more resistant than the Americans to the idea of AEAF domination, has in fact thrown himself whole-heartedly into the battle, has improved his bombing performance enormously, and has contributed more to the dislocation of enemy communications, etc., than any of the rest.

Bomber Command carried out some 55 operations in support of the Allied armies in June, of which 32 were against rail centres. The number of operations dramatically decreased in July, with only 18 against rail targets.

EVENTS

1. 1956hrs–2034hrs. Eighth Air Force's Bombardment Divisions are ordered to strike their targets more or less simultaneously. The 1st Bomb Division (108 B-17s) divides south-east of Dreux, with six Groups heading for the railway centre at Massy-Palaiseau and another three Groups for Juvisy. Bombing results are reported as being fair to good. This force loses only one aircraft, B-17 *Stormy Angel*, which is hit by flak and goes down near Rouen on the way home.

2. 2042hrs–2128hrs. The 3rd Bomb Division (B-17s) targets the western Parisian railway centres at Achères and Versailles. Eighty-two Fortresses attack Achères, with good results and only one B-17 is lost, which eventually explodes over Maisons Laffite.

3. 2043hrs–2122hrs. The 2nd Bomb Division crews assigned to Versailles find the target cloud-covered and make for the secondary target, the airfield at Conches on the other side of Paris, which is attacked with only fair results.

4. 2048hrs. The attackers which suffer most are the 72 B-24s of the 2nd Bomb Division, which attempt to bomb Brétigny airfield. One is destroyed on the bomb run west of Brétigny, while another crashes near Jossigny. Only 12 of the 76 B-24s actually bomb Brétigny. The remainder fly on and bomb Creil airfield to the north of Paris.

5. 2048hrs–21.44hrs. Three more B-24s go down on the way home: *Stubby Gal II* goes down over Creil and two others crash near the coast. All have succumbed to flak. This comparatively low loss rate is almost certainly due to the massive escorting forces assigned to the bombers. Seven Fighter Groups provide close escort to and from the targets. Meanwhile, another Group of P-38 Lightnings patrol the vicinity of Évreux, covering the bombers' withdrawal from the south. A group of Mustangs near Compiègne perform a similar function, covering the area to the north. A sweep by P-47s to the south-east fails to 'flush out' any Luftwaffe fighters. The Luftwaffe simply could not afford to defend the French railways in the face of such overwhelming odds.

Eighth Air Force Mission 385, 2 June 1944

In the early evening of 2 June 1944, the US Eighth Air Force dispatched 319 bombers against four railway centres of the Parisian *Grande Ceinture*. The massive escorting fighter force was an effective deterrent and this mission, like several before it, served to confirm Spaatz's prediction that the Luftwaffe would refuse to defend the French railways.

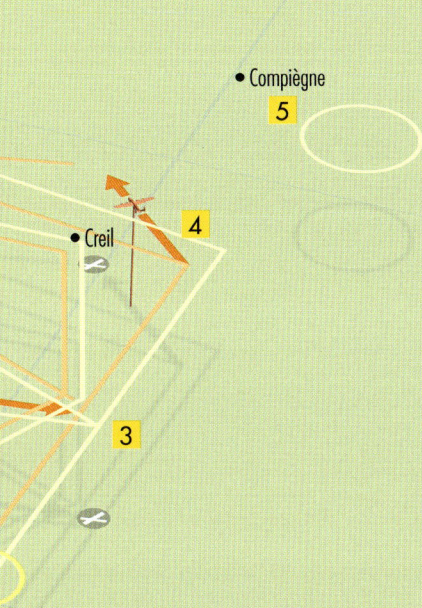

Key:

 Allied bombers

Escort fighters

 Railway yards/stations

 Axis airfields

The leading *Nachtjagd experte*, Heinz Wolfgang Schnaufer of NJG1. On the night of 24–25 May, he successfully entered the bomber stream attacking Aachen, where he shot down five bombers in just 14 minutes. Bomber Command losses for the raid came to 25 aircraft; the *Nachtjagd* was still a potent force. (INTERFOTO/Alamy Stock Photo)

Bomber Command's accuracy continued to be problematic. The marking for the attack on 9–10 June on the rail junction at Étampes was accurate but late, the bombing spreading into the town, killing 131 people. Three nights later, attempts to hit Cambrai and Caen ended with badly scattered bombing across both towns. Cambrai and Douai were hit again the following night, when haze or partial cloud, coupled with the loss of the Master Bomber over Douai, hampered accurate bombing.

Poor conditions forced Master Bombers to halt some raids before they were completed, notably on Aulnoye and Montdidier on 17–18 June and on Revigny on two consecutive nights, 12–13 and 13–14 July. By this point, emboldened by the feeble resistance offered by the Luftwaffe's day fighters, Bomber Command was bombing again by day – although visibility was still a problem. A daylight attack on Vaires on 12 July was stopped by the Master Bomber after only 12 Lancasters had bombed. Other attacks attained better results: Poitiers was badly damaged on 12–13 June by No. 5 Group, and efforts against the rail yards at Limoges and Saintes on 23–24 June and Vaires on 27–28 June were also praised.

The loss rate continued to rise, skewed slightly by the losses incurred on the nights of 7–8 June (28 losses, 8.3 per cent), 15–16 June (11 losses, 4.9 per cent), 28–29 June (20 losses, 8.7 per cent) and 30 June–1 July (14 losses, a terrifying 11.9 per cent). The July loss rate was 3.1 per cent. This figure was badly affected by a disastrous attack on 18–19 July against Aulnoye and Revigny marshalling yards, in which 26 from a force of 253 bombers were lost – 10.3 per cent.

The Eighth Air Force made fewer attacks, and by July it had more or less fully resumed the offensive over Germany. This does not include unofficial 'sweeps', in which returning escort fighters searched for targets of opportunity over France and Germany. The AEAF air forces concentrated on the interdiction campaign after D-Day, although this included tactical attacks by medium bombers on a large number of smaller stations, junctions and yards. Meanwhile, the elaborate programme prepared for Luftflotte 3's reinforcement had broken down in the face of overwhelming Allied air superiority. Although Luftflotte 3 tripled in size in the days following the landings, by 30 June its fighter strength was down to 37 per cent of establishment, only 49 per cent of which were operational.

The Allied Expeditionary Air Force

The majority of medium bomber participation in the campaign was carried out by the Ninth Air Force. It was expected that the near-simultaneous attack of the targets allocated within each block would serve to multiply the transportation problems in that area. The bombing proficiency of the Ninth's medium bombers was praised; in May, accuracy was further improved by the new tactic of flights of six aircraft flying on converging lines of attack over targets. Many of the tactical bombers' missions were attacks on railway centres already struck by Bomber Command to maintain pressure on the repair efforts. The most heavily attacked yard was at Creil, 27 miles north of Paris. This target, a major centre and junction for east–west rail traffic, was hit 11 times before D-Day. Others struck repeatedly in their respective allocation blocks were Béthune (attacked eight times), Arras, Namur and Valenciennes; Aulnoye, Mézières-sur-Seine and Aarschot; Mons, Mantes-Gassicourt and Busigny. Overall, between 1 March and 5 June, the medium bombers of the Ninth Air Force attacked 36 rail centres 139 times.

Although opposition was usually light from both flak and fighters, this was not always the case. On 27 May, two combat boxes of A-20 Havocs from the 409th Bomb Group mounted a mission against Amiens. When only some 27 miles from the target, intense flak suddenly rocked the Group, immediately downing one of the three aircraft in the lead group. Within minutes, a second A-20 in the same group was hit. It was seen gliding earthwards before a wing broke off and the aircraft plunged into the ground. The flak then damaged an engine on the remaining lead aircraft, which turned back before the crew was eventually forced to abandon the aircraft. The lead formation then broke up, some returning to base, while others either joined the second formation or struggled on alone. Apart from the loss of three aircraft out of the 19 in the formation, only two A-20s escaped without damage: a testament to the effectiveness of German flak on formations flying at medium altitude in clear visibility.

Overall, the medium bombers of the Ninth Air Force played an important, if somewhat forgotten, role in the campaign against the rail centres. Despite a very considerable number of sorties flown, their contribution is overshadowed by Bomber Command on one side and on the other by the starring role played by the fighter-bombers.

B-26 Marauders of the Ninth Air Force, bomb doors open, approach the Namur rail centre. As the campaign progressed, Brereton ordered smaller and more compact attacking formations of six aircraft each, which resulted in tighter bomb groupings and enhanced accuracy. (Bettmann/Getty Images)

OPPOSITE THE US NINTH AIR FORCE FIGHTER-BOMBER BRIDGE ATTACK TECHNIQUE

The pre-D-Day Transportation campaign effort on rail centres by Air Force, 6–7 March–5 June 1944		
Air Force	Tonnage dropped	Percentage effort by tonnage
Bomber Command	46,712	66%
Eighth Air Force	10,008	14%
Second TAF	1,919	3%
Ninth Air Force	9,444	13%
Fifteenth Air Force	3,074	4%
Total	71,157	

The post D-Day Transportation campaign effort on rail centres by Air Force, 6 June–early August 1944		
Air Force	Tonnage dropped	Percentage effort by tonnage
Bomber Command	32,436	65%
Eighth Air Force	8,545	17%
Second TAF	1,088	2%
Ninth Air Force	4,794	10%
Fifteenth Air Force	2,844	6%
Total	49,707	

The Seine railway bridge at Vernon following the attack of 7 May 1944. Although the operation was rightly hailed as a triumph, bridges, especially masonry examples, remained difficult to cut. In the end, it was the medium bombers of the Ninth Air Force which enjoyed the greatest bridge-cutting success. (Crown Copyright, MoD)

The tactical campaign

Solly Zuckerman accepted the importance of tactical attacks on rail traffic in the days before D-Day, predominantly by fighter-bomber sweeps against those trains still running. What Zuckerman did not propose was the type of interdiction campaign suggested by the EOU in March, targeting road and rail bridges and supply depots. Zuckerman and Leigh-Mallory had argued against attacks on bridges from the start. Evidence seemed to prove that, in general, a bridge was too small and too strong to make a worthwhile target; the rail experts calculated that heavy or medium bombers would need to drop 1,200 tons of bombs per bridge destroyed. Additionally, there were too many bridges over the Seine and Loire to destroy in the limited time available. Finally, their flak defences would probably make more accurate medium- or low-altitude attacks prohibitively costly. Those bridges damaged were thought relatively easy to repair. Zuckerman concluded that 'only a direct hit counted on a bridge, whereas any bomb on a railway centre caused damage'.

The need for a tactical phase of the pre-*Overlord* campaign was primarily the concern of Montgomery's 21st Army Group. Their proposals gradually evolved until by early April they called for tactical attacks to begin from D-20 on road and rail

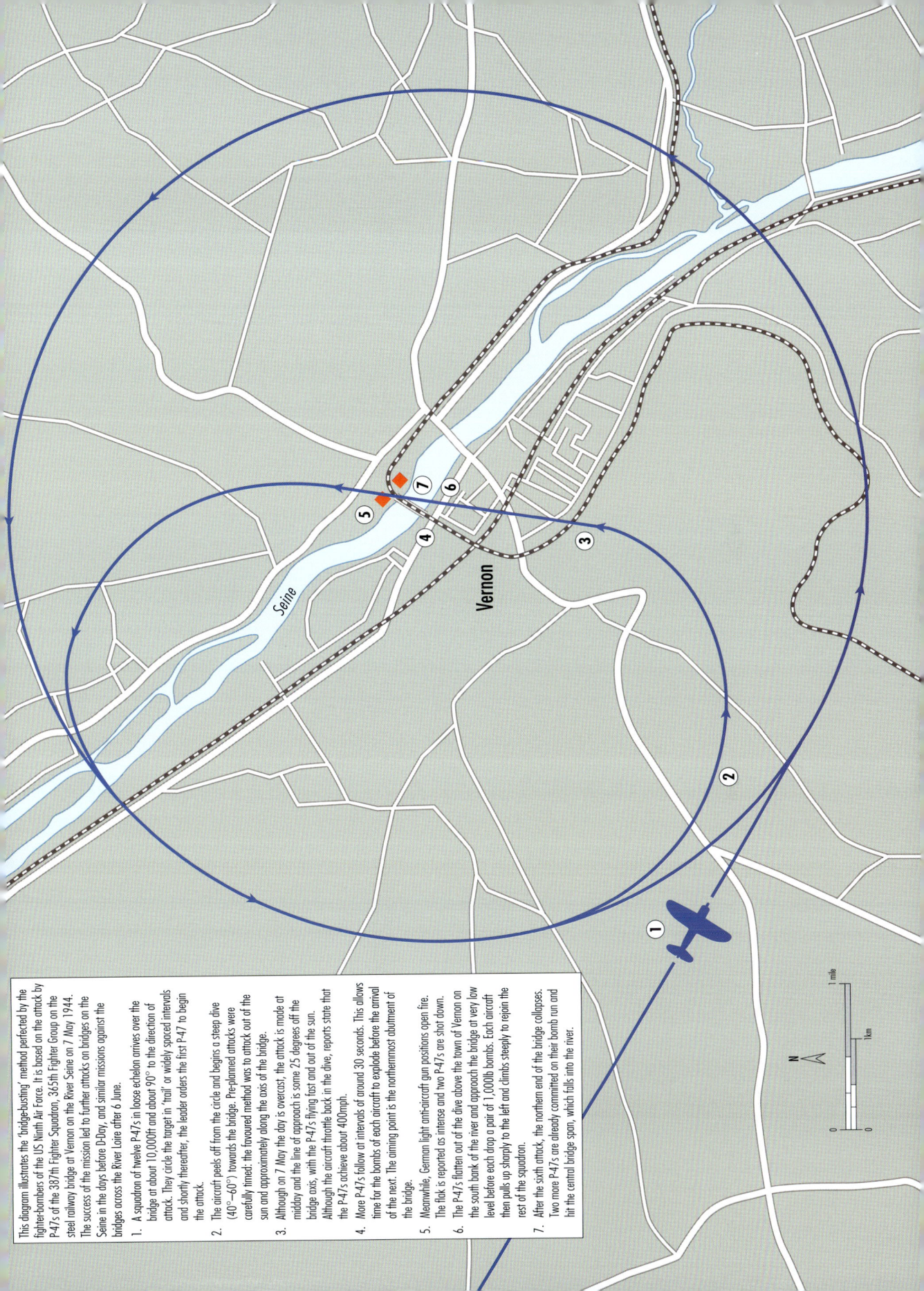

bridges, junctions and chokepoints (small towns and villages). Specifically, five bridges on the Seine were chosen for air attack. By 19 April, a more detailed version of the plan, 'Tactical Attacks on Rail Communications', admitted that the complexity of the French road network offered few locations for worthwhile roadblocks. The best opportunities were offered by lines of interdiction on the Seine and Loire bridges. A few weeks later, the overall air plan seemed to envisage tactical 'rail cutting' being made after D-Day. Meanwhile, as already related, the idea for attacks on bridges had been given a full study by the EOU. Their proposal, for a short but intensive campaign on bridges and supply dumps, in tandem with an oil campaign, was the dual scheme which Spaatz had failed to broach on 25 March.

Despite Zuckerman's scepticism, the pressure for a full bridge interdiction campaign resurfaced in mid-April, when the results from Operation *Strangle* – medium bombers and fighter-bombers had 'knocked out' 27 Italian bridges – filtered through to London. That month, Air Marshal Sir John Slessor, the RAF commander in the Mediterranean and Middle East, wrote to Portal:

> One of the most remarkable developments in the past three months to my mind has been the emergence of the bridge as a worthwhile bombing objective… I have always thought the bridge was a rotten objective – and so indeed it was in the past. The explanation of the change is twofold; first, the astonishing accuracy of the medium bomber groups – particularly the Marauders … secondly, the accuracy of the fighter-bomber in the low attack. I hope the value of the bridge as an objective in attack on communications is thoroughly realised by the Tactical Air Forces in UK – it is something new since Tedder's day out here.

Spaatz, having visited Italy, returned convinced by the evidence offered by medium bombers and fighter-bombers. The tactical air force trio of Coningham, Brereton and Quesada were also supportive of a bridge interdiction campaign. On 25 April, Hawker Typhoons had used bombs and rocket projectiles to badly damage river bridges in the Cherbourg area. On 6 May, the question came up again at a meeting of AEAF commanders. In many accounts, Leigh-Mallory is shown as remaining averse to the idea of bridge attacks by medium bombers or fighter-bombers. The minutes of the meeting suggest otherwise. After Coningham had proposed experimental attacks on bridges, Leigh-Mallory 'said that it was worth trying out between now and D-Day what was the most effective method using mediums and fighter/bombers'. The Ninth Air Force made its first attack on the Seine bridges the next day, when P-47 Thunderbolts destroyed the rail bridge at Vernon and badly damaged that at Mantes-Gassicourt.

Follow-up attacks were made over the next four days on Mantes-Gassicourt, which was destroyed, and on the Seine bridges at Mézières (cut by P-47s and P-51s), Oissel (two bridges attacked by B-26s, one destroyed) and Orival (damaged by Typhoons). Heartened by this success, on 10 May Leigh-Mallory ordered further attacks to be made. The plan of attack proposed three lines of interdiction, with at least one point on each railway route to be attacked on each interdiction line, thus sealing the battle area absolutely. The first line ran south-east along the Seine, then to Beaugency and finally westward along the line of the Loire. Twenty-seven bridges across this line were chosen for attack. The second line ran east of Paris, from Étaples on the coast to Clamecy south-east of Orléans. The third line of interdiction, which stretched through Belgium and on to the Swiss border at Belfort, was not systematically attacked. For security, early attacks concentrated on the bridges on the River Meuse and the Albert Canal; attacks on the Seine bridges and the Paris–Orléans Gap were suspended until 24 May (D-13). Those on the Loire were attacked only after D-Day. Map 3 on page 42 shows the progress of the interdiction campaign from May until July 1944.

The interdiction campaign

Much has been made of the bridge cutting campaign, and the accuracy of the tactical air forces' fighter-bombers and medium bombers, but as with the rail centres, the bombing of bridges was subject to a number of factors:

1. The size and construction of the bridge. The longer the bridge, the easier it was to hit. Stone and concrete bridges were found to be more durable that those of steel construction.
2. The weather conditions during the attack.
3. The type of aircraft employed. Fighter-bombers offered greater accuracy than medium bombers, which in turn were better than the high-altitude bombers of the Eighth Air Force.
4. The enemy defences, primarily flak.
5. The extent and urgency of the subsequent repair effort. The German authorities accorded greater priority to certain crossing points than others. Repaired bridges needed to be attacked again to maintain the line of interdiction.

By D-Day, the seven Seine bridges selected from Mantes near Paris to the sea had been rendered impassable. Below Mantes, where the Seine entered the heavily populated Paris suburbs, there were too many bridges to make attacks worthwhile, and although some were attacked, the bombing programme against them was sporadic and half-hearted. After D-Day, the Germans concentrated on rebuilding the bridges at Oissel and Le Manoir, and these were cut and re-cut a total of five times.

The interdiction campaign before 6 June 1944 (bomb tonnage)				
	Heavy bombers	Medium bombers	Fighter-bombers	Total tonnage
Seine bridges	0	1,755	561	2,316
Loire bridges	0	0	0	0
Tonnage dropped	0	1,755	561	2,316

After D-Day, the bridge campaign spread to the gap section between Paris and Orléans, where 2,700 tons of bombs were aimed at ten bridges. Overall, 17 'cuts' were achieved, four by fighter-bombers and 13 by mediums. However, the gap was not struck as regularly or as heavily as it perhaps should have been, and there was evidence that it continued to provide a relatively healthy supply route into Normandy.

Hell Hawks!

On 7 May 1944, 12 P-47 Thunderbolts of the 387th Fighter Squadron, 365th Fighter Group, USAAF, set course for the railway bridge which spanned the River Seine in the picturesque town of Vernon. Each of the P-47s was armed with two 1,000lb bombs, fitted with 8–11-second delayed fuses. Identifying their target through a break in the clouds, the first Thunderbolts began their attack. By the time that the third pair of Thunderbolts, *The Turnip Termite* flown by Capt Arlo Henry and *The Madam* of 1st Lt John Fetzer, began their attack run, it seemed to them that every flak gun in Vernon was waiting for them. Henry, with Fetzer 50yds behind, dived from 10,000ft and levelled out at full throttle and 400mph over the town, making for the northernmost abutment.

Henry dropped his bombs and climbed away to safety. As the northern end of the bridge loomed up, Fetzer toggled his bomb release. Then disaster struck: Fetzer's starboard bomb detached successfully but the port-side one hung up. Immediately, *The Madam* tipped onto her port wing, just feet above the river. As Fetzer's Thunderbolt screamed past the northern abutment, one of Henry's bombs exploded, throwing chunks of masonry into *The Madam* and blasting her over the bridge. Although badly damaged, Fetzer managed to jettison the hung-up bomb before evading more flak and returning to base 'on the deck'. *The Madam*, despite needing two new wings, a new tail, new engine and new supercharger, would fly to the end of the war.

The fourth pair of Thunderbolts collapsed the north end of the bridge, before more bombs brought down the centre span for good measure. This attack vindicated the bridge-cutting lobby's claims, but such attacks did not work against all types of bridge and many still required repeated attacks by large numbers of medium bombers.

On 8–9 June 1944, the Saumur tunnel was attacked by No. 617 Squadron. One Tallboy bomb caved in the roof of the tunnel mouth, visible on the far right. The movement of the 17th SS Panzer-Grenadier Division was delayed and the tunnel was not repaired before the Battle of Normandy was over. (Crown Copyright, MoD)

An intensive campaign began against the Loire bridges. No less than 4,300 tons of bombs were aimed at the Loire, 2,650 tons in the nine days to 15 June. All eight of the Loire bridges selected were cut, though not at the same time. Repairs were attempted on six of these, and on five these efforts were successful. Repair work was frequently interrupted by air attacks, most of which were by medium bombers from the Ninth Air Force. The Loire campaign reached a peak of intensity during the American breakout from St Lô (Operation *Cobra*), in order to protect the flank of the US Third Army as it turned east.

Of note is the attack on 8 June by 617 Squadron Lancasters on the rail tunnel at Saumur. Nineteen Tallboys (deep-penetration medium-capacity bombs, weighing six tons apiece, designed to demolish the sturdiest structures) were dropped and one succeeded in caving in the tunnel entrance. The tunnel was not cleared until late July, by which time the bridge over the river to the north had been cut anyway. Equally impressive was the case of the Loire bridge at Ponts de Cé near Angers. One span of the bridge had been cut as long ago as 1940, but had still not been repaired by June 1944. Feverish repair work began on 8 July, and by the morning of 19 July was complete. The bridge was cut that same afternoon. Repair work resumed, and on 31 July the bridge was again ready. Before any traffic passed, it was attacked on the same day and again on 1 August, at which point the repair effort ceased. The ten Loire bridges (the eight originally selected and the two noted above) were cut a total of 27 times by fighters and medium and heavy bombers.

The Val Benoit bridges over the Meuse at Liège after attacks by B-26s of the Ninth Air Force on 25 and 28 May 1944. Although the bridges were damaged, some of the bombs inevitably fell on the town. The Meuse attacks fulfilled the twin aims of Operation *Fortitude* and the Interdiction Plan. (Crown Copyright, MoD)

Attacks against the 21 bridges on the second line of interdiction began after D-Day. Systematic attacks did not begin until mid-July and it was not until after the St Lô breakout that attacks were stepped up. Hence, the second interdiction line served less to hinder supplies going into Normandy than to hamper the subsequent German retreat. The second line interdiction attacks in the north were markedly less successful than those on the first line, mainly due to the smaller average length of the bridges – just 90ft. The seven bridges in the eastern part of the second line, averaging 210ft in length, lent themselves better to air attack. On 25 June, in an effort to impede the progress of the 9th and 10th SS Panzer Divisions, all seven bridges were attacked by the Eighth Air Force. The attacks were made in good visibility and were fairly accurate: two bridges were permanently closed to traffic and three temporarily. These bridges were reattacked twice more in July and August. Some of the most successful attacks were those against the three bridges on the upper Loire section of the second line. These, with an average length of 1,200ft, made pinpoint accuracy less of an issue, and two of the three were permanently closed after a single attack.

The interdiction campaign after D-Day, 6 June–August 1944 (bomb tonnage)				
	Heavy bombers	Medium bombers	Fighter-bombers	Total tonnage
Seine bridges	265	471	110	846
Loire bridges	2,899	1,255	144	4,298
Tonnage dropped	3,164	1,726	254	5,144

On average, the tonnage required per bridge cut accorded with the pre-campaign expectation. The table below shows the results of the different methods of attack during the campaign as a whole.

The interdiction campaign: bridge cuts achieved, May–August 1944 (bomb tonnage)				
First line of interdiction	Fighter-bombers	Medium bombers	Heavy bombers	Total
Rouen to Mantes-Gassicourt (Seine)	4	8	1	13
Mantes to Beaugency (Gap section)	4	13	0	17
Blois to Nantes (Loire)	3	11	9	23
Total first line cuts	11	32	10	53
Second line of interdiction	5	5	17	27
Cuts grand total	16	37	27	80
Tonnage dropped per cut	83	163	239	

The 'Chattanooga Choo Choos'

The strafing of rail and road traffic had occupied a minor role in the Zuckerman Plan. An informal policy of ground-attack missions had of course been a long-running feature of Allied fighter operations over Europe. However, concerns over civilian casualties by strafing trains and road transport, and the bombing of open stretches of line and small railway stations, had led to official discouragement of such attacks over much of the campaign. On 20 May, Leigh-Mallory permitted large-scale fighter-bomber sweeps to begin over the tactical area: the region bordered by the Seine to the north-east and to the south by a line connecting the Seine with Évreux, Chartres, Le Mans and Rennes. Eighth Air Force fighters were permitted to sweep a zone 50–100 miles wide on the tactical area's periphery. Two weeks after D-Day, the tactical area was expanded to include the Brittany peninsula and areas north of the Seine and east of Paris. The air forces eagerly seized their opportunity, and an orgy of destruction over France, Belgium and western Germany followed.

The missions in this phase of the campaign varied. Some were simply fighter sweeps, in which targets of opportunity were attacked. Others were armed reconnaissance sorties over

A train under the guns of an American fighter. From 21 May 1944, Allied fighters were given free rein to attack rail traffic across France and Belgium. The result was a massive fighter sweep, known as 'Chattanooga Choo Choo' day. More Chattanoogas were flown before D-Day, including over Germany and even Poland. (Imperial War Museums, FRE 3343)

specific areas. On occasion, the participants were briefed on particular targets or railway lines, and at other times the mission commander chose the area or target to be attacked. Strafing was usually combined with bombing and targets varied widely: locomotives, freight wagons, tank wagons and even infrastructure. Water towers in rail yards were an obvious favourite. Additionally, targets such as supply depots, radar stations, airfields and motor vehicles were attacked on the same missions.

About 18,500 sorties were flown by the tactical air forces against such targets, 2,700 in the two weeks before D-Day and 15,800 over the remainder of the campaign. The Ninth Air Force accounted for over 33 per cent of sorties. Eighth Air Force fighters attacked rail targets on many sorties across France and Germany when providing escort to the bombers. These sorties were probably as numerous as those flown by the tactical air forces.

The best-known anti-transportation fighter sweeps were the famous 'Chattanooga Days', the first of which took place the day following the lifting of the ban on 21 May. Surviving but incomplete SNCF records reveal that over 113 locomotives were damaged on 21 May. On the same day, Eighth Air Force fighters claimed to have damaged an even greater number of locomotives in western Germany. The first Chattanooga was followed by five more before D-Day. On 25 May, the sweeps again focused on France, with the Eighth venturing into Germany. Four days later, a sweep was made across Germany and even into Poland. Three more, on 2, 3 and 4 June, concentrated on the tactical area around Normandy.

The strafing was immediately successful. On 26 May, the German authorities ordered a reduction in daytime traffic on lines subjected to strafing, forcing a greatly increased proportion of traffic to be moved by night. During periods of actual strafing, French crews were known to leave their locomotives untended on open lines, and German crews began to be used on the more hazardous routes. In the two weeks before D-Day, almost 500 locomotives were damaged by strafing, while a further 1,000 were damaged during the remainder of the campaign. Impressive though these figures are, the actual efficacy of strafing locomotives was doubtful. Many pilots returned with gleeful reports of columns of

The Tempest hits Europe

After 20 May 1944, the Allied air forces began a phase of intensive strafing and bombing attacks against trains across France, Belgium and Germany. Allied planners estimated that the bombing of the major railway centres selected by the Transportation Plan had cut down almost all French civilian rail traffic, leaving those trains that were still running carrying German supplies. On 21 May, the US air forces carried out a massive train-strafing fighter sweep across France, which became known as the first of the 'Chattanooga Choo Choo Days'.

The following day, Wing Commander Roland Beamont led a formation of three new Hawker Tempest Mk Vs on a train-busting sweep across northern France. After crossing the coast, the pilots soon found a train approaching the marshalling yard at Lens. The three Tempests strafed the train, then re-formed and flew on.

Shortly afterwards, smoke was seen from a train near Orchies. Diving from 1,200 to 400ft, Beamont opened fire at the locomotive from a range of 700yds. The 20mm cannon shells blasted the hapless locomotive, which immediately, in Beamont's words, 'brewed up'. Meanwhile, a light flak gun mounted on a flat car at the rear of the train opened fire at Beamont's Tempest. The gun was attacked and suppressed by *Blue 2*.

The Tempests found and strafed two more targets. Beamont attacked a single locomotive entering the small goods yard at La Bouverie by rolling his Tempest inverted and diving at 45 degrees. Another train was spotted near a hamlet on the coast and attacked at roof-top height by all three Tempests.

The number of locomotives that were actually destroyed by the Allied fighter sweeps from May 1944 is open to question. However, reports from the SNCF stated that French locomotive crews refused to serve on the more hazardous routes, forcing the German authorities to draft replacement crews from the *Deutsche Reichsbahn*.

This mission was one of the first by the Hawker Tempest over Europe. Beamont would make many other such sweeps during the campaign before eventually being shot down by flak on 2 October, becoming a PoW until the end of the war. In 1947, he joined the fledgling English Electric company in Preston, Lancashire, later part of the British Aircraft Corporation, where he tested a series of aircraft, notably the Canberra and Lightning.

Wing Commander Roland Beamont, 1944. Beamont gained a mass of experience in the Battles of France and Britain, and later with the Hawker Typhoon. In early 1944, he took command of the first Tempest Wing; the sweep he led on 21 May was one of the first made by the Tempest over Europe. (Crown Copyright, MoD)

steam escaping from ruptured locomotives, although such impressive visuals could be generated by the locomotive crews hurriedly reducing boiler pressure. According to Obst Hans Höffner, CO of *General des Transportswesens West*, between ten and 15 locomotives a day were strafed, and these were usually repaired in eight days. More work was required if the boiler had burst, rather than only the tubes being punctured. Altogether, Höffner calculated that 20 per cent of the strafed locomotives were irreparable.

Mention should also be made of line cutting, in which bombs were dropped on small stations or even open stretches of line by fighters and medium bombers. Altogether, 8,000 tons of bombs were dropped in these missions, producing about 1,000 track cuts by the end of July. This considerable, if unsystematic, effort was concentrated in *Regions Ouest* and *Nord*. Fighters flew the bulk of the sorties, but about one-third of the total tonnage was dropped by medium bombers, mainly against small stations. Cuts or blockages were ranked in importance as follows: rail centres, bridges and cuts on open stretches of line. Ultimately, the unsystematic nature of the rail-cutting campaign clouds any realistic assessment of its effectiveness.

The Resistance contribution

Contributions were also made by the Resistance, which helped by destroying stretches of line, sabotaging points and signalling equipment and derailing locomotives. As a rule, the cuts or blockages produced usually lasted under a day and were therefore of only minor inconvenience. Other more subtle forms of sabotage were practised. One example is the sabotaging during May of the rail flat cars at Montauban near Toulouse, earmarked for the movement of the Tiger tanks of the 2nd SS Panzer Division Das Reich. With great bravery, a small number of very young French resisters repeatedly stole into the sidings where the flat cars were hidden. Over the month, the oil in the axle boxes was drained and replaced with an abrasive powder supplied by a local SOE agent. The axles duly seized, delaying the movement of the 2nd SS Panzer Division's tanks to Normandy.

The German reaction

On 15 May, the German Transport Ministry produced a gloomy analysis of the situation:

> In the occupied areas of the West, particularly in Belgium and northern France, the raids carried out in recent weeks have caused systematic breakdown of all main lines; the coastal defences have been cut off from the supply bases in the interior, thus producing a situation which threatens to have serious consequences … large-scale strategic movement of German troops by rail is practically impossible at the present time, and must remain so while attacks are maintained at the present intensity… In assessing the situation as a whole it must further be borne in mind that, owing to the widespread destruction and damage of important construction and repair shops, the maintenance and overhaul of locomotives has been considerably disorganised; this causes further critical dislocation of traffic.

Bombs fall from B-26 Marauders over the Ponts de Cé bridge on the Loire, 1 August 1944. The repeated cutting of this and other bridges across the Loire by the Ninth Air Force played a vital part in the German defeat in Operation *Cobra*: the US breakout from Normandy at St Lô. (Imperial War Museums, EA 30877)

This was followed on 3 June by a similarly pessimistic Luftwaffe report:

> The systematic destruction that has been carried out since March of all important junctions of the entire network – not only of main lines – has most seriously crippled the whole transport system (railway installations, including rolling stock). Similarly Paris has been systematically cut off from long distance traffic, and the most important bridges over the lower Seine have been destroyed one after another… It is only by exerting the greatest efforts that purely military traffic and goods essential to war effort, e.g. coal, can be kept moving.

The report added that the wrecking of facilities in *Region Ouest* 'has been so successfully achieved, locally at any rate, that the *Reichsbahn* authorities are seriously considering whether it is not useless to attempt further repair work'.

The first German armoured reinforcements were ordered to move towards Normandy on D-Day itself. Transport issues came to the fore immediately. Höffner complained that 'considerable damage had been done to the roadbed throughout the northwestern part of France adjoining the Belgian border, a number of the Meuse bridges had been destroyed, and railroad capacity had shrunk considerably'. When the Seventh Army began to redeploy divisions on 7 June, truck requirements were 20 times the number that was available. In general, German units – both armoured and infantry – arrived in the battle area in small elements and were often committed into the line in a piecemeal fashion. The following armoured divisions are given in the order in which they are considered to have reached the battle area.

Vernon was the location for both a rail and a road bridge. Both were cut in the attacks of May and June 1944. By August, Allied troops were at the Seine. A bulldozer is seen being ferried across, with the damaged road bridge, still impassable, in the background. (Imperial War Museums, BU 196)

- The 21st Panzer Division was already based in Normandy and entered combat on D-Day.
- The leading units of the 12th SS Panzer Division arrived on D+1, although shortages of transport hampered its arrival.
- Between 8 and 10 June, elements of the crack Panzer Lehr Division were gradually fed into the battle from their base near Le Mans.
- The 17th SS Panzer-Grenadier Division, based south-west of Tours, lacked transport and was delayed by the destruction of the Saumur railway tunnel on 8 June. Despite this, it entered combat between 10 and 14 June.
- The notorious 2nd SS Panzer Division was not combat-ready on 6 June, being especially short of transport (partly due to the actions of the Resistance). It travelled very slowly from north-east of Toulouse, with delays caused by the bombing of Limoges and Saintes. The tanks crossed the Loire over the only rail bridge capable of taking them (Tours la Riche), using ropes to haul them across. Some of the tanks

had to move by road for the greater part of the distance, due to the inability of the railroad to bring back SS flatcars from north of the Loire to the entraining stations. It eventually arrived in Normandy over an extended period stretching well into July.

- One of the best German armoured formations, the 2nd Panzer Division, left its base near Amiens on 11 June and took nine days to arrive. The unit's motor transport travelled via Paris.
- The bulk of the two armoured divisions on the Eastern Front earmarked for the invasion in the West, the 9th and 10th SS Panzer Divisions, detrained at Nancy, with only the tanks proceeding by rail. The rest of the units travelled by road, and it is estimated that while the 1,000 miles between the start point and Nancy was covered in only five days, due to the untouched German rail network, the 350 miles from Nancy to the battle area took another nine days.
- The 1st SS Panzer Division, based near Ghent, was incomplete and not combat-ready on 6 June. This unit was ordered to move on 8 June but did not begin to do so for another nine days. The journey should have taken about three days but the division became badly delayed, probably due to the bombing of the rail centres at Ghent, Lille and Maubeuge shortly after its move began, and was eventually forced to detour around Aachen and Nancy. The unit was reported to have detrained west of Paris on 25 June, and elements of it did not join the battle until 6 July.
- Two armoured divisions effectively missed the main battle. The first was the 116th Panzer Division, which, in need of re-equipment and training on D-Day, only entered the battle at the end of July. The 9th Panzer Division, incomplete and short of vehicles after service in the East, was eventually diverted to the south of France and hence missed the Normandy fighting.

Five infantry divisions were moved south from the Pas de Calais and Belgium. One which travelled via Paris ran into severe congestion and was delayed. The rest moved to Rouen by rail at a rate of eight trains per day. Of these, two which unloaded at Rouen are known to have been ferried over the Seine.

Allied and German build-up of divisions after D-Day (Source: Zuckerman collection, AEAF 1/13: 'An Appreciation of the results up to D+30', 25 July 1944)		
	Allied divisions landed	German divisions in battle area
D+4	16	11
D+7	19	15
D+14	23	17
D+17	24	18

Worsening matters was the competition between troop trains and supply trains. After the early arrival of the first three panzer divisions, at no time were the German units able to prepare a *Schwerpunkt*, a concentrated blow against the Allied line. The supply situation for the German forces in Normandy deteriorated markedly to mid-June, mainly due to the sheer number of extra units increasing the supply burden. To worsen matters, there is no evidence that any supply trains crossed the Seine or the Loire. Allied air superiority forced supplies onto the inadequate truck reserve. Movement was carried out at night, where more road accidents occurred in the darkness. In June, Army Group B lost a staggering 4,200 vehicles it could ill-afford.

By mid-June, the Germans realised that Normandy could only be held by restoring rail routes. Early uncoordinated repair efforts were abandoned and work concentrated on reopening (and keeping open, despite frequent air attacks) two arterial routes into Normandy: the Paris–Versailles–Dreux–Surdon line from the east and the Tours–Le Mans–

Alençon–Sees–Surdon line from the south. More lines reopened in late June and these are shown on Map 3:

23 June: Le Mans–Sable–Sègre–Redon–Quimper and Nantes–Rennes–Dol.

28 June: Saumur–Château du Loir–Le Mans and Nantes–Angers–Le Mans.

The fuel supply, never healthy, had all the makings of a disaster by the middle of June. By 13 June, the entire fuel reserve had been sent to Normandy. The 'Berta' fuel depot near Domfront was destroyed by air attack on 13 June; ten days later, the largest depot in the West, near Gennevilliers north of Paris, was destroyed and over 600,000 gallons of fuel were lost. The ammunition supply told a similar story: by mid-June, the Seventh Army had expended 5,000 tons of ammunition but received only 3,000 tons.

In late June, the German logistical situation began to improve, for the following reasons:
1. Railway lines into Normandy were reopened.
2. Ferrying operations on the Seine were begun and by July were transporting about 20 per cent of all supplies arriving in Normandy.
3. Units began to send their own vehicles to collect supplies from the forward depots.

The situation on the German eastern flank in Normandy improved and the Anglo-Canadian efforts to push south-east and capture Falaise were halted. However, on the western flank, opposite St Lô, there was little improvement. Supply trains did not cross the Loire as often as they did the Seine. Between 9 June and 7 July, only 33 per cent of supplies to western Normandy and 40 per cent of Seventh Army's fuel passed through the Tours railway centre. Then, as related, a series of disasters struck the Seventh Army's logistical network. The Loire rail bridges were attacked again, and the important St Cyr bridge at Tours was cut. Tours itself was heavily damaged in mid-July, and by the eve of Operation *Cobra*, only the single-track Port Boulet rail bridge remained open over the Loire. Fuel depot 'Bruno' at Châteaubriant was destroyed on 16 July and fuel deliveries fell by 22 per cent. When the St Cyr rail bridge was reopened on 23 July, it was too late for the launch of Operation *Cobra* on 25 July. By the eve of *Cobra*, the formations defending St Lô had only enough fuel for about two days of heavy combat. Ammunition was equally short; by the end of the first day of *Cobra*, the German defenders had expended all the ammunition for the 88mm guns which formed the backbone of its anti-tank defence.

Assessing the course of the campaign

The Intelligence Section at Allied Supreme Headquarters (SHAEF G-2) provided a series of weekly summaries on the campaign's progress. On 13 May, the report gave a reasonably optimistic summary, noting that in the western German yards recently attacked by the Eighth Air Force, the repair work was fast and efficient. On the other hand, it was admitted that part of this evaluation rested on a 'highly coloured' German press article – a less than reliable source. The summary then considered recent attacks on the French and Belgian centres, notably Ghent, Lens, Courtrai, Lille and other centres in eastern France. By this stage, traffic towards the north coast from the south and especially the east was being routed south of Paris, avoiding the badly damaged centres in north-east France and Belgium. It was noted that little effort was made in the majority of cases to repair heavily bombed centres, other than one or two through-lines. The exceptions were Reims and Troyes, both of which were working again within a week and handling much of the aforementioned westbound traffic.

By 3 June, SHAEF G-2's mood had changed. This report, compiled on the eve of D-Day, painted a less sanguine picture. It was estimated that the French and Belgian railway system had suffered the destruction or blocking of some 5,400 locomotive services and the destruction or damage of 1,700 locomotives and 25,000 wagons. However, 'French traffic has invariably been curtailed at the expense of German requirements… Consequently the actual losses of locomotives, servicing facilities, wagons and line capacity are not such

The railway bridge over the Loire at Orléans under repair in late 1944. Engineers have used the old bridge supports for a new temporary structure. The Loire bridge campaign played a key role in the German collapse in front of St Lô in July 1944. (Roger Viollet via Getty Images)

that the enemy will be prevented from moving up supplies and reinforcements as required, although such movement will be less efficiently operated.' The report gave a damning verdict: 'Evidence as to the effect on German troop movements remains unsatisfactory but the effects till now do not appear to have been very serious.'

It was very difficult to assess the real effectiveness of the bombings as the campaign unfolded. A mass of information, some of it very valuable, came in the form of reports from France and Belgium, either from civilians via Allied agents or from pro-German propaganda newspapers and radio broadcasts. In any event, these sources – especially the latter – were subject to an element of bias. Nevertheless, information from within Occupied Europe was fragmentary and difficult to piece together, it could help to build an overall picture.

More rigorous Allied analysis depended for the most part on photo-reconnaissance. Although such sorties were comprehensive, there was only so much information that could be gleaned from post-raid imagery. The 'train count' of certain centres could be estimated over time, and the approximate number of locomotives and stock destroyed could therefore be gauged. Damage to facilities and the length of time taken to repair main lines could also be assessed. Yet physical damage was not a sound criterion for judging enemy military movements, and it was not until the campaign was effectively over at the end of July that the interrogation of personnel and captured documents could allow a full analysis.

AFTERMATH AND ANALYSIS

French women take cover, Caen, July 1944. Although the air attacks on Caen were not part of the Transportation Plan, their effect on French civilians was much the same as earlier attacks. Ironically, after D-Day was launched, the concern shown by Churchill and others over French civilian casualties ceased. (DPA Picture Alliance/Alamy Stock Photo)

The dust had not settled when the claims over the success or otherwise of the campaign began. The battle lines drawn in the spring of 1944 between Tedder and Zuckerman on the one hand, and almost everyone else on the other, were to powerfully inform the future judgements on the campaign.

This examination of the campaign and its aftermath will briefly consider the conclusions drawn at the time by the various interested parties, before studying the consequences for the German reinforcement and supply of the battle area in Normandy during June and July 1944. The impact of the campaign on the subsequent Allied war effort will be assessed and finally the longer-term legacy on later campaigns.

The Allied view

The *United States Strategic Bombing Survey Summary*, produced in September 1945, was based on comprehensive assessments of damage, mainly to economic targets within Germany, and it had little to say about the Transportation campaign. The American official history, *The Army Air Forces in World War II*, was cool in its praise for the strategic campaign but considered the Interdiction Plan to have been successful. The authors noted that comments made on the campaign by Germans under interrogation varied, while captured French and German documents could be interpreted to support several points of view. The history also mentioned that in June 1944, SHAEF's G-2 had deemed the campaign a disappointment. The Ninth Air Force's two studies made it clear that while the strategic bombing had made little difference, interdiction had been decisive, a view shared by Kindelberger's Enemy Objectives Unit. Another AAF report – a lengthy and meticulous study of the campaign – judged that the effort expended on rail centre bombing could have been put to better use.

The British post-war bombing survey, written under Zuckerman's aegis, unsurprisingly attributed considerable credit to the pre-*Overlord* strategic campaign against the rail centres. The post-D-Day campaign, in which tactical attacks by heavy bombers were intended to

In this image taken in September 1944, an American military policeman near Alençon waves on a 'Red Ball Express' truck convoy taking priority materiel to the forward areas. The damage to the French rail network forced the American armies to partially rely on motor transport for the advance across France. (American Photo Archive/Alamy Stock Photo)

block selected chokepoints, was of less interest to Zuckerman. The British post-war survey made the following points:

1. In *Region Nord*, the volume of originating traffic, expressed in wagon-loadings, began to fall steeply about the middle of March. By 26 May (before the destruction of the Seine bridges), it had fallen to 20 per cent of the previous peak level.
2. The attacks had almost as great an effect on traffic circulating between France, Belgium and Germany as they did on internal French rail traffic. The French *Regions* were unable to accept a large proportion of even the highest-priority traffic originating from outside the country.

3. *Region Nord* received about 20,000 tons of bombs; *Region Ouest* about 10,000 tons.
4. Therefore, two to three months of bombing had paralysed the economic life of France.
5. The survey admitted that the rail centre offensive did not affect German troop movements as dramatically as it did French non-military and German economic traffic. Yet Zuckerman stated that German troop trains had slowed to a 'trickle' in the first two weeks after D-Day.

Zuckerman was dismissive of the interdiction campaign, pointing out that since attacks on bridges depended on good weather conditions, there were periods in which the maintenance of the lines of interdiction was impossible. The Seine bridges were cut for most of the post-D-Day period, but there were very few days when one or two railway bridges over the Loire could not be crossed. On most days, at least 50 per cent of the bridges in the second line of interdiction were usable. Zuckerman claimed that the lack of traffic passing over the bridges was not due to their being destroyed or damaged; rather, it was the damage to the railway centres which had reduced the number of available trains.

It may be thought that the debate would end there: the post-war bombing surveys were wound up, their findings published and the world moved on. However, Tedder and Zuckerman left their own memoirs, both of which defended the rail centre campaign strongly and at length. The only major riposte came much later, when in 1981, the EOU's Walt Rostow wrote a slim book in which he too retold the events leading up to the campaign. It need hardly be said that Rostow was not an admirer of Zuckerman, and much of the book deals with the development of the rival oil campaign and the effect it had on Germany's defeat.

An American locomotive unloading at Cherbourg, August 1944. To compensate for the French locomotives requisitioned by Germany or destroyed in the Transportation campaign, the Allies brought their own: between D-Day and early October, 1,300 locomotives, 37 ambulance trains and 20,000 freight wagons were unloaded in France. (Keystone-France/Gamma-Rapho via Getty Images)

Rostow took the view that the bridge campaign was more successful than the rail centre campaign. His reasoning was much as it had been in 1944: the amount of effort needed was smaller; it left the strategic bombers free to pursue more important targets (namely synthetic oil refineries) and the cost in civilian lives was far smaller.

The German view

In one of his post-war interrogations, Obst Hans Höffner, CO of General des Transportswesens West, thought that the bombing of rail centres affected French civilian traffic more than it did German traffic, partially due to the setting-up of auxiliary marshalling centres. That the campaign caused a locomotive shortage (which was always regarded as an incidental effect) is evidenced by the allocation of at least 200 locomotives from Germany to France in June and July. The situation was made more difficult by the destruction of locomotive repair sheds, but this was partially addressed by stopping locomotive production and converting the larger factories to repair work. The average daily running distance of serviceable locomotives declined by over 50 per cent from the norm of 120km, mainly as a result of the increase in waiting time caused by difficulties in rail dispatching and congestion.

Höffner compared the interdiction campaigns on the Seine and the Loire, remarking that 'the capacity of the Loire bridges, roughly eight trains per day on the average, was roughly equal to the total capacity of the isolated area north of the river'. The large amount of traffic crossing the Seine meant 'the Loire bridges were less of a bottleneck than the limited capacity of the area to the north'. Nevertheless, the interdiction of the Loire bridges served to produce serious difficulties. While the Seine routes were almost sufficient for the units holding the eastern flank of the Normandy front, the difficulties experienced on the Loire fatally undermined the German position opposite St Lô. For Höffner, the bridge campaign was 'a first-class calamity'.

It is probably true to say that, although the strategic and tactical elements of the Transportation campaign did not prevent or fatally undermine the German reinforcement of the Normandy area, they did allow the Allies to gain a decisive advantage in the build-up race. More serious was the effect on the German logistical chain as the battle went on. The Seine bridge campaign, while effective in hindering reinforcements crossing the river in the first weeks, was undermined by the use of ferries to move supplies during late June and July. The Loire campaign, on the other hand, was almost an inverse: formidable German units, including the 17th SS Panzer-Grenadier and 2nd SS Panzer Divisions, were able – albeit with difficulty – to cross the Loire shortly after D-Day. Yet by mid-July, the cutting of bridges across the river had combined to fatally weaken the fuel and ammunition supply situation in the western part of the German line. The exact causes of the logistical disaster (for that was what it was) which gripped the German units in Normandy are hard to separate from one another: ultimately, the effects of rail centre and interdiction campaigns, as some post-war studies admitted, merged into one another.

In the medium-term, the campaign had two important effects. The first was the need to repair extensive sections of the rail network. Although this was achieved for the American armies, reliance on the famous 'Red Ball Express' – the massive logistical effort made by the US Army's lorries – has put this achievement in the shade. Even as the Allies drove across France, the debate on the best employment for the strategic bombers over Germany was reignited. With the Luftwaffe on its knees, Spaatz had been pursuing his oil offensive and Harris was anxious to return to his previous campaign on the German cities. Tedder's proposal, which owed much to Zuckerman, was to restart the Transportation campaign, this time extending it into Germany. This was not aimed at the hampering of troops and supplies but rather the dislocation of the entire German war economy, by crippling the transport infrastructure which supported it. This primarily aimed at the transport of coal, the lifeblood of the German industrial economy. The resulting 'communications' campaign put a severe strain on the German economy, at a time when the Third Reich was collapsing from a variety of pressures. In the longer term, the Normandy Interdiction Plan informed the later campaign in Korea. The Fifth Air Force's commander stated that as far as interdiction was concerned, the same style of plan as used in World War II was adopted in the later conflict.

The question of casualties

The original estimate of between 80,000 and 160,000 French civilian casualties was mercifully wide of the mark. Zuckerman himself, using data computed from experience gained in the Blitz, calculated a figure of 12,000 dead and 6,000 injured from the rail centre campaign. By late April, the interpretation of available evidence suggested that casualties had been about half the number feared.

Zuckerman's figures were inaccurate. It is difficult to be certain of the exact numbers, but French civil defence figures are: 712 dead in March, 5,144 in April, 9,893 in May and an estimate of 9,517 in June. While this total of 25,266 is not complete, the figures are for the bombings over France as a whole and not all of the casualties stemmed from the bombing of railway centres. Ironically, the considerable anxiety shown by Churchill and the British government over the casualty question seemed to be forgotten once the Allies landed. Efforts to produce roadblocks or to pave the way for Allied attacks by the brutal bombings of some Norman towns, especially Caen, attracted almost no comment. Casualties suffered in the heat of battle were seemingly borne with greater equanimity.

However, the casualties sustained across France and Belgium were in part due to the use of Bomber Command – the least accurate of the Allied air forces – over targets which required a high degree of precision. Despite the improvements in accuracy made in the course of the campaign, Harris's Command still remained a bludgeon. The attack on Noisy-le-Sec covered 30km^2, while that on Lille, which opened this book, spread over 32km^2. Probably the worst attacks were those made in daylight by the Fifteenth Air Force on 26 and 27 May. The first, on St Étienne, was reasonably accurate but killed more than 1,084 people. A raid on Marseille the following day was scattered across the city and killed 1,752. Neither city had been in a war zone and the provision of shelters was inadequate.

In January 1944, Harris wrote: 'Long experience of night operations has shown that it is impossible for night bombers working individually to carry out a successful and concentrated attack on even a large and clearly defined target, except under conditions of excellent visibility, bright moonlight and meagre opposition.' Many histories have backed Tedder's argument that events showed Harris to be confounded by the virtuosity of his own crews. Instead, given the casualties imposed by the strategic bombing of the railway centres, Harris's early prediction should perhaps be reconsidered.

The debates over the relative success of the campaign's strategic and tactical elements, or its moral standing, will probably never be settled. Those involved stuck to their arguments to the end. The Allies, by air power and elaborate deception, won the 'battle of the build-up' in Normandy and their opponents were ultimately unable to assemble the forces necessary to drive them out of France. Whether the Battle of Normandy, and the subsequent course of the war, would have been different if there had been no Transportation campaign, or either just a strategic or an interdiction plan, lies safely in the realm of counterfactual history.

FURTHER READING

Secondary sources

Note: Although many of the works listed below are now out of print, some are readily available in digitised format.

AAF Evaluation Board, European Theatre of Operations, *Effectiveness of Air Attack Against Rail Transportation in the Battle of France* (1945)

Churchill, Winston S., *The Second World War, Volume 5: Closing the Ring*, Houghton Mifflin, Cambridge (1951)

Craven, Wesley & Cate, James, *The Army Air Forces in World War II, Volume Three*, Office of Air Force History, USAF, Washington DC (1983)

Davis, Richard G., *Carl A. Spaatz and the Air War in Europe*, Center for Air Force History, Washington DC (1993)

Gilbert, Martin and Arnn, Larry P., *The Churchill documents Volume 19: Fateful Questions, September 1943 to April 1944*, Hillsdale College Press, Michigan (2017)

Hart, Russell A., 'Feeding Mars: The Role of Logistics in the German Defeat in Normandy' in *War in History*, Vol 3, No 4 (November 1996)

Mark, Eduard, *Aerial Interdiction: Air Power and the Land Battle in Three American Wars*, Center for Air Force History, Washington DC (1994)

Middlebrook, Martin & Everitt, Chris, *The Bomber Command War Diaries, 1939–1945*, Pen & Sword, Barnsley (2021)

Mierzejewski, Alfred C., *The Collapse of the German War Economy 1944–1945: Allied Air Power and the German National Railway*, University of North Carolina Press, Chapel Hill (1988)

Murray, Williamson, *Luftwaffe*, The Nautical and Aviation Publishing Company, Baltimore (1985)

Pogue, Forrest, *Cross-Channel Attack*, Center of Military History, US Army, Washington DC (1993)

Pogue, Forrest, *The Supreme Command*, Center of Military History, US Army, Washington DC (1989)

Price, Alfred, *Instruments of Darkness: The History of Electronic Warfare, 1939–1945*, Frontline Books, Barnsley (2017)

RAF Air Historical Branch, *The Liberation of North West Europe Vol I: Planning and Preparation of AEAF for the Landings in Normandy*, Stanmore, Middlesex

RAF Air Historical Branch, *The Liberation of North West Europe Vol III: The Landings in Normandy*, Stanmore, Middlesex

RAF Air Historical Branch, *The RAF in the Bombing Offensive Against Germany Vol VI: The Final Phase March 1944–May 1945*, Stanmore, Middlesex

Rostow, W.W., *Pre-Invasion Bombing Strategy: General Eisenhower's decision of March 25, 1944*, Gower, Aldershot (1981)

Tedder, Lord, *With Prejudice*, Little, Brown, Boston (1966)

Terraine, John, *The Right of the Line*, Hodder & Stoughton, London (1985)

The Strategic Air War Against Germany 1939–1945, Report of the British Bombing Survey Unit, Frank Cass, London (1998)

United States Strategic Bombing Survey Summary Report (European War), Air University Press, Maxwell AFB, Montgomery, Alabama (1987)

Various, *The Combined Bomber Offensive, 1 January to 6 June 1944*, AAF Historical Office (1947)

Various, *The Ninth Air Force in the ETO, 18 October 1943 to 16 April 1944*, Assistant Chief of the Air Staff, Historical Division (1945)

Various, *The Ninth Air Force in the ETO, April to November 1944*, Assistant Chief of the Air Staff, Historical Division (1945)

Webster, Sir Charles & Frankland, Noble, *The Strategic Air Offensive Against Germany 1939–1945, Volumes III & IV*, HMSO, London (1961)

Zetterling, Niklas, *Normandy 1944: German Military Organization, Combat Power and Organizational Effectiveness*, Casemate, Oxford (2020)

Zuckerman, Lord, *From Apes to Warlords*, Hamilton, London (1978)

Primary Sources

The University of East Anglia

The Zuckerman Archive

The National Archives

AIR 37: various documents

The Royal Air Force Air Historical Branch, Northolt

Appendices to *The Liberation of North West Europe Vol I: Planning and Preparation of AEAF for the Landings in Normandy*

The Royal Air Force Museum, Hendon

Lord Tedder papers, Vincent Orange Collection

INDEX

Note: page numbers in **bold** refer to photographs, illustrations and captions.

AEAF (Allied Expeditionary Air Force), the 6, 8, 12–13, 31, 32, 35, 37, 45, **45,** 50, **56,** 65, 68, 69, 72
after-mission reports 4, **45,** 58
Air Ministry Intelligence 40
air raid warning leaflets **46**
air superiority 7, 8, 9, 12, 20, 36, 37, 49, 68
air-to-air refuelling 11
aircraft
  Avro Lancaster (UK) 4, **5,** 16, 34, **38,** 56, 58, 59, 62, **63,** 68, 76
    R5868 'S-Sugar' **64**
  Boeing B-17 (US) 18, **19,** 51
  Consolidated B-24 Liberator (US) 19, **19,** 51, 63, 64
  de Havilland Mosquito (UK) 4, 16, **31,** (53)**54–55,** 56, 58, 59
  Douglas A-20 Havoc (US) **49,** 69
  Focke-Wulf Fw 190 (Germany) **16,** 25
  Handley Page Halifax (UK) 4, 16, 33, 34, **38,** 53, **55,** 58, 59, 62, **68**
  Hawker Tempest (UK) 13, **16,** (79)**80–81**
  Hawker Typhoon (UK) 9, **10,** 13, 72, **82**
  Junkers Ju 88 (Germany) 25, 26
  Lockheed P-38 Lightning (US) 14–15, **15,** 19, 64
  Martin B-26 Marauder (US) 14, **62, 69,** 72, **77, 83**
  Messerschmitt Me 109 (Germany) 25
  Messerschmitt Me 110G (Germany) **21,** 25, 26
  Messerschmitt Me 210 (Germany) 63
  North American P-51 Mustang (US) 14, 18, 19, 25, **39,** 64
  Question Mark (experimental plane) 11, **20**
  Republic P-47 Thunderbolt (US) 9, 14, **15,** 18, 19, 26, 72, (73)**74–75**
  Short Stirling (UK) 16, **17,** 33
  Supermarine Spitfire (UK) 13, 64
Allied strategy **4,** 5, 6, **7,** 7–9, 12, **12,** 18, 18–20, **19,** 21, 31–33, 35–47, **41, 49,** 49–62, **51–52,** 64–65, 68, **69,** 70–82, **73, 77, 85,** 86, 91–92
ammunition supplies 26, 30, **49,** 86, 91
anti-aircraft fire **15,** 16, 17, 63, 69, (73)**74–75,** (79)**80–81**
flak defences 22, **26,** 26–27, 70, 73
Armée de l'Air, the 21–22, 27
Arnold, Gen Henry 'Hap' 11, **12,** 20
Atlantic Wall, the **30**
Atlee, Clement 46

BBC, the 27
Beamont, Wing Cmdr Roland **79, 82**
Bedell-Smith, Walter 35
Bennett, Air Vice Marshal Donald 16, **16,** 56
blind-bombing aids 17, 20
bomb ordnances 4, 16, 34, 47, 62, 65, 70, **70,** 73, **73,** 76, **77,** 78, 82, 90
bomber formations 19, 69, **69**
bombing accuracy 5, 9, 17, **17,** 19, 21, 22, 53, 56–57, 59, 62, **62, 63,** 64, 68, 69, **69,** 72, 73, **77,** 92
bombing raids 8, 9, **15,** 18, 21–22, **49, 51–52,** 53, 60–**61,** 63, 66–**67,** 68, 69

Amiens 69
Angers 59
Berlin 15
Cherbourg 9
Creil 69
Hamm 63
Hasselt **62, 64**
Juvisy **43,** 58, **58, 59**
La Chapelle 9, 59
Le Mans **44**(**45**), 45, 53, 62
Leipzig 16
Liege 64
Lille 4–5, **5**
Louvain 62
Malines 59
Namur **69**
Nantes junction 62
Noisy-le-Sec 58–59
Region Nord, Aulnoye **8,** 53, **56,** 68
Tergnier 59
Tours 58, **63,** 86
Trappes **8, 48,** 53, (**53**)**54–55**
Villeneuve St Georges 4
Bradley, Gen Omar 14, **35**
Brant, E. D. 12, 32
Brereton, Lt Gen Lewis 12, 14, **14, 69,** 72
bridge-cutting attacks 9, **10,** 4**2**(**43**)**, 70,** (**70**)**71,** 70–76, 86, 91
and the Interdiction Plan 7, 8, 14, 40, 41–43, **42**(**43**)**,** 68, 70, 72–78, **73,** (**73**)**74–75, 76, 77, 78,** 88, 89, 90, 91–92
on the Loire and Seine 9, 70, 72, 73, **73,** 76, 77, **77, 78, 83,** 86, **87,** 90, 91
Saumur rail tunnel 76, **76,** 84
Vernon 9, **70,** 72, (**73**)**74–75, 84**
bridge-rebuilding 30, **87**
British Bombing Survey Report, the **12**
Bufton, Air Cmdor Sidney 45, 47

Cairo Conference, the 35
Cheshire, Wing Cdr Leonard 43
Churchill, Winston **4,** 5, 6, 8, 9, 10, 12, **33, 34,** 35, 38, 39, 45, 46–48, **88,** 92
civil defence in France 27
Cochrane, Air Vice Marshal Hon Ralph 17, **17**
Combined Bomber Offensive, the 6, 7, 11, 50
command channels and hierarchies 6, 8, 35, 38, 39–40
Coningham, Air Chief Marshal Arthur 10, 11, 13, 14, **14,** 72
COSSAC (Chief of Staff to the Supreme Allied Commander) 10, **31**

damage assessment 88
deaths 5, 7, 21, 53, 62, 64, **64,** 65
of civilians 31, **35,** 45, 46, 47–48, 53, 59, 68, 78, **88,** 91, 92
Deutsche Reichsbahn, the 24, **79,** 83
Dickens, Sir Basil 38
Doolittle, Gen James 18, **18, 19,** 20
Dray, Fly Off A. A. **53**(**54–55**)

Eaker, Gen Ira 11, 18
Eden, Anthony 45, 46
Eisenbahnflak (flak trains), the 26
Eisenhower, Gen Dwight D. 6, 8, 9, 10–11, **13,** 31, 34, 35, **35,** 38, 39, 40, 43, 45, 47, 50
engines 13, 14
  Napier Sabre 13

EOU (Enemy Objectives Unit), the 7, 8, 12, 32, 40, 41, 43, 47, 70, 72, 88, 90–91

Fetzer, 1st Lt John **73**
fighter-bomber support 12, 14
fighter-bomber sweeps 9, **16,** 64, 68, 70, 78, 79, **82**
  Chattanooga fighter sweeps **39, 78,** (**79**)**80–81,** 79–82
fighter escorts 19, 41
fighter *experten* 68
Finlay, Flt Lt W. G. (**53**)**54–55**
Freemasons, the 22
French and Belgian railways, the 6, **8,** 9, 21, 22–24, **23,** 30, 33, 34, **44**(**45**), 45, 50, **51–52,** 53, 85–86, **89,** 91
French anti-aircraft units 22, 26
fuel supply 29–30, **49,** 86, 91
Gaulle, Gen Charles de 20
Gebietsverkehrsleitung West (Area Traffic Management West), the 24
General des Transportwesens West, the 24
German Army, the 27, **28,** 29, **29,** 77, 83–85
  1st SS Panzer Division 85
  2nd SS Panzer Division 82, 84, 91
  9th SS Panzer Division 85
  10th SS Panzer Division 85
  17th SS Panzer-Grenadier Division **76,** 84, 91
  21st Panzer Division 84
  I SS Panzerkorps 29
  Seventh Army 29–30, 83, 86
German defence strategy 21, 24–29, **28(29), 30,** 40, 63, 64, 82–85, **85,** 88, 91
German industrial capacity 37, 43
  synthetic oil refineries 8, 18, **19,** 41, 45, 63, 91
German reinforcements 24, **25,** 34, 46, 68, 83, 87, 88, 91, 92
ground marking aids 17, 58
  'Musical Newhaven' 58
  No. 5 Group marking method 9, (**56**)**57,** 58, 62
  Oboe (blind-bombing device) 17, 53, 58, 59, 62
  TIs (Target Indicators) **53,** 58, **58,** 59
Guderian, Heinz 29

Harris, Air Chief Marshal Sir Arthur 6, 7, **11,** 13, 15, 16, 17, 35, 36–**37, 37,** 40, 43, 50, 53, 56, 58, 91, 92
heavy bombers 4, 5, 6, 17, **17, 22,** 36, 38, 41, 45, 47, 50, 70, 73, 76, **77, 78, 78,** 88–89
Henry, Capt Arlo **73**
Hitler, Adolf 27, 29
Höffner, Obst Hans 82, 83, 91
Hughes, Lt Col Richard D'Oyly 12, 32, 37, 40
HVD (*Hauptverkehrsdirektion*), the 24

intelligence 11–12, 40, 41, **45,** 86–87
and photo-reconnaissance 12, 50, **59,** 87
Italian railways, the 32, **32,** 37

Kaysen, Carl 12
Kindelberger, Charles 12, 88
Koenig, Gen Pierre-Joseph 20, **35**

Lawrence, Oliver 11, 43
Leigh-Mallory, Air Chief Marshal Sir Trafford 6, 9, 13, **13,** 32, 34, 35, 36, 37, 38, 43, 53, 65, 70, 72, 78

INDEX

Lindemann, Prof Frederick (Lord Cherwell) 12, **33**, 45–46
locomotive supplies **90**, 91
logistics and supply 29–30, **49**, 85–86, 91
Luftwaffe, the 6, 7, 8, 10, 11, 18, **18**, 21, 26, 36, 37, 43, 45, **47**, 64, 83
   JG (Jagdgeschwader)
      JG 1 64
      JG 2 25
      JG 26 25
      III./JG 26 64
   Luftlotte 3 24, 25, 64, 68
   Luftlotte Reich 64, 65
   NJG *(Nachtjagdgruppen)* 25–26, 63, **65**
      NJG 1 **68**
      NJG 4 25

marching distances 30
Master Bomber, the 59, 62, 68
matèriel losses 8, 9, 15, **15**, 16, 17, 18, 25, 41, 43–45, **53, 62**, 63, 65, 68, **68**, 69, 85, **90**
medium bombers 9, 12, 14, 27, 41, 50, 52, 68–69, 70, **70**, 72, 73, **73**, 76, **77, 78**, 82
MEW (Ministry of Economic Warfare), the 11–12, 40, 41, 43
military strength and complements 29, **29**, 68
Montgomery, Field Marshal Bernard 10, **13**, 70
morale 16, **17**, 18
night operations **5**, 17, 36, 46, 53, **(53)**54–**55**, 56, 58, 59, 62–63, **65**, 68, **68**, 92
Norden gyroscope-stabilised bombsight, the 19

Oesau, Obst Walter 64
Oil Plan, the 8, 41, 43, 45, 72, 91
Operations
   Argument (February 1944) 7, 18
   Blazing 6
   Cobra (July 1944) 9, **83**, 86
   Corkscrew (June 1944) 6
   Crossbow (December 1943 – May 1945) 6
   Fortitude (December 1943 – March 1944) 49, **77**
   Overlord (June 1944) 5, 6, 10, 14, 18, 33, 36, 37, 38, 39, 43, 49–50
      preparatory phase 49, 50
   Steinbock (January – May 1944) **47**
   Strangle (March – May 1944) 6, 72
OSS (Office of Strategic Services), the 12, 20

Pantelleria **7**, 12
Park, Air Vice Marshal Keith 13
pathfinder units 36
performance 14, 16, 19, **31**
personal tensions 10, 13, **13**, 14, **14**, 37, 38, **41, 43**
Pointblank directive, the 5, 6, 7, 15, 21, 36, 37, 39, **41**, 43, 49
Portal, Air Chief Marshal Sir Charles 8, 11, **11**, 13, 16, 34, 36, 38, 39, 43, 46, 72
post-war surveys and analyses 88–92
precision bombing 19–20, **62**
production 8, 14, 16, 18, 30, 33, 41, 43, 63, 91
propaganda 27, 47, **47**, 87

Quesada, Lt Gen Elwood 'Pete' 11, 14, **20**, 72

radar systems
   Flensburg (Germany) 25

H2S (UK) 17, 20, 25
H2X (US) 19
Lichtenstein SN-2 (Germany) **21**, 25–26, 63
Naxos (Germany) 25
RAF, the 27, 47
   2nd TAF (Tactical Air Force) 12, 13, **14**, 64, **70**
   AI (Air Intelligence) 12
   Bomber Command 6, 8, 9, 11–12, 15–18, 20, 21, 33, 34, 35, 36–38, **37**, 39, **45**, 46, **48**, 50, **51**, 53, **53**, 56, 58, 59, **60–61, 62**, 63, 65–68, 69, **70**, 92
   No 2 Group 12
   No 3 Group 16, **17**, 59, 62
   No 4 Group 16
   No 5 Group 17, **17, 43**, 56, 58, 68
   No 6 Group 59, 62, **65**
   Pathfinder Force 15, 16, **16**
   CIU (Central Interpretation Unit) 12
   Desert Air Force 10
   Fighter Command (Air Defence of Great Britain) 12, 13
   Middle East Command 11
   Official History 16, 17
   PRU (Photographic Reconnaissance Unit) 12
   squadrons 56
      No 61 Sqn **5**
      No 105 Sqn **31**, 53
      No 109 Sqn **(53)**54–**55**
      No 467 Sqn **64**
      No 486 Sqn **16**
      No 617 Sqn 17, **43**, 76, **76**
RAF Museum, Hendon **64**
rail-cutting 82
ranges 14, **15**, 19, 33
rate of fire 26
'Red Ball Express' truck convoys **89**, 91
repair trains 30
repairs 30, **39**, 40, **45**, 76, **76**, 82, 85–86, 87, **87**, 91
Resistance, the 20, 82
Rommel, Feldmarschall Erwin 29, **30**
Roosevelt, F. D. R. **4**, 5, 6, 9, 10, 35, 47, 48
Rostow, Walt 12, 43, 90–91
RRS (Railway Research Service), the 12, 32
Rundstedt, Feldmarschall Gerd von **27**, 29

sabotage 20, 47, 82
Schnaufer, Heinz-Wolfgang **68**
Schwerpunkt, the 85
Securité Aérienne Publique (Public Air Safety), the 27
SHAEF (Supreme Headquarters Allied Expeditionary Force), the 10, 20, 31, **31**, **51**, 65
   SHAEF G-2 (Intelligence Section) 86–87, 88
Sherrington, C. E. R. 12, 32
Sicilian railways, the 6
Slessor, Air Marshal Sir John 72
SNCF (Société nationale des chemins de fer français), the 6, 22–24, 79, **79**
   Region Nord **8**, 24, 82, 89, 90
   Region Ouest 24, **44(45)**, 82, 83, 90
   Region Sud-Ouest 24
SOE (Special Operations Executive), the 20
Spaatz, Gen Carl 'Tooey' 7, 8, 9, 10, 11, 12, **12**, 14, **18, 19**, 20, 35, 36, 37, 38, 40, 41, **41**, 43, 45, 50, 51, 63, 72, 91
Sperrle, Generalfeldmarschall Hugo 24

Stalin, Josef **4**, 5
'Study No. 6: The Delay of Enemy Reserves during the Initial Stages of Neptune' 6, 31–32

tanks
   Panther (Germany) **25**
   Tiger (Germany) 82
Tedder, Air Chief Marshal Sir Arthur 6, 7, 8, 9, 11, 12, 13, **13**, 15, 31, 34, **35**, 36, 37, 38, 39, **41**, 43, 45, 46, 47, 72, 88, 90, 91–92
Tehran Conference, the **4**, 5, 6
Toohey, Francis J. 11
training and experience 14, 16, 21, 25, **26**, 27, 58, 63
Transportation Plan, the 5, 6, 7, 8, 9, **11, 12, 32**, 32–34, **38**, 40, 43, 45–46, 47, 49, 56, 63, 64, 65, **70, 79, 88, 90**, 91–92
   variant A 33
   variant B 33

US Third Army, the 76
USAAF, the 7, 11, 12, 18, 27, 47
   Bomb Groups
      381st **19**
      409th 69
      458th **19**
      482nd **19**
   Eighth Air Force 6, 9, 11, 14, 15, **15**, 18, 21, 33, 35, 43, 47, 51, **51–52**, 63, 64–65, **66–67**, 68, **70**, 77, 78, 79
   Fifteenth Air Force 18, 35, 38, 51, **70**, 92
   Fighter Groups
      364th **15**
      365th **15**, **(73)**74–**75**
   Ninth Air Force 9, 11, 12, 13–14, **14**, 15, **15**, 35, **49, 52, 62**, 69, **69, 70**, **(70)**71, 72, 76, **77, 83**, 88
   XIX Fighter Command 14
USSTAF (US Strategic Air Forces), the 11, 12, 18, 20, 35, 36, 38, 41, 43, 50

Vichy France 27

War Cabinet Defence Committee, the 8, 9, **34**, 45–47
War Office Intelligence 40
weaponry
   20mm Flak 38 (Germany) 26, 27
   30mm cannon (Germany) 26
   37mm Flak 36 (Germany) 26, 27
   37mm Flak 43 (Germany) 26
   .50cal machine gun (US) 14, 18
   88mm anti-aircraft gun (Germany) 26, **26**, 86
   Tallboy bomb (UK) 76, **76**
   V-1 flying bomb (Germany) 6, 36
weather conditions 17, 19, 20, 53, **53**, 59, 62, 64, 68, 90

Zuckerman, Solly 6, **7**, 10, 12, **12**, 15, 31–34, **32**, 36–37, 40, **41**, 43, **45**, 46, 65, 70, 88–89, 90, 91, 92